APES AND ANGELS

*Those who wish to degrade man to beast,
caricature him to the rank of the orang
outang; and, in idea, raise the orang
outang to the rank of man.*

J. K. Lavater
Essays on Physiognomy

APES AND ANGELS

The Irishman in Victorian Caricature

L. Perry Curtis, Jr.

David & Charles : Newton Abbot

ISBN 0 7153 5239 3

Published in England by David & Charles, Ltd.
Distributed in the United Kingdom, the traditional British market,
and Europe by David & Charles, Ltd., South Devon House,
Newton Abbot, Devon, England

Published in the United States by the Smithsonian Institution Press
Distributed in the United States and Canada by George Braziller, Inc.,
One Park Avenue, New York, New York

Typeset by Western Printing Services Ltd, Bristol
Printed by Latimer Trend, Whitstable

Contents

	Preface	vii
	Acknowledgments	xi
I	Physiognomy: Ancient and Modern	1
II	The Ethnology of Irish Celts	16
III	Victorian Comic Art	23
IV	Simianizing the Irish Celt	29
V	Irish-American Apes	58
VI	Irish Angels	68
VII	Fenian Physiognomies	89
VIII	The Cartoonists' Context	94
	Notes	109
	Selected Bibliography	118
	Index	123

Preface

WHAT'S IN A FACE? What's in a caricature of a face? How were the physical features of a man, especially those of the face, supposed to reveal both character and temperament? How and why did Victorian comic artists use the facial angle devised by Camper to denote degrees of civility, intelligence, and morality as well as race? These are some of the questions which this study of Irish faces in Victorian political cartoons and caricature seeks to answer. The gradual but unmistakable transformation of Paddy, the stereotypical Irish Celt of the mid-nineteenth century, from a drunken and relatively harmless peasant into a dangerous ape-man or simianized agitator reflected a significant shift in the attitudes of some Victorians about the differences between not only Englishmen and Irishmen, but also between human beings and apes. This volume explores the connections between Victorian images of the Irish, the lore of physiognomy, the Darwinian debate over evolution, and the art of caricature. In looking so closely at the serious side of comic art, we run the risk of neglecting the warm humor and wit of nineteenth-century cartoons. The comic content of cartoons, on the other hand, is notoriously difficult to translate into words. Cartoons are meant to be seen, not read about in secondhand versions. In spite of Wordsworth's still timely warning that "we murder to dissect," this study has focused upon certain peculiar features in political cartoons relating to the Irish question and Irishmen during the reign of Queen Victoria. Hopefully, the illustrations in this volume will compensate in part for what has been lost on the dissecting table. But even if there is no substitute for the reproduction of every cartoon mentioned here, we have at least tried to treat cartoons not as amusing frivolities which burst like soap bubbles at a glance, but as historical documents which contain many valuable clues about the societies which produced and enjoyed them.

This inquiry started out several years ago as a brief glimpse of Irish faces in English political cartoons from the 1860s to the early 1900s. It soon became clear, however, that anyone who wanted to make sense of the subject had to venture beyond the congenial task of turning over the pages of *Punch* and *Judy*. It was necessary to work in comparative terms: to compare what happened to Irish features in cartoons after 1860 with what went before, to compare English stereotypes of Irish faces with English stereotypes of English faces and then do the same for Irish stereotypes in cartoons, and to compare the dominant images of the Irish people in cartoon and caricature with the realities available in contemporary photographs. In other words, the complexities and perplexities of the subject increased at a compound-interest rate.

Generalizations about the images entertained by one national or ethnic group about another ought to invite some scepticism under the best of conditions. The present study is not based on a random sample of cartoons gathered from every region or city in the British Isles, and it does not attempt to quantify the intensity of feelings of the "in-group" towards the "out-group" with or without the specious precision of some social psychologists and sociometrists. It does seek to identify and explain a few of the more striking features of that cluster of attitudes and assumptions which made up the image of the Irish Celt in Victorian England and Scotland as a creature not fully civilized and not quite human. A trans-Atlantic perspective is given to the subject by a brief look at Irish-American features in several comic weeklies published in New York City. Because men of science, letters, and the arts all played some part in assembling and sustaining the simianized image of Paddy, this discussion will range from classical humoralism to Victorian ethnology and caricature, the connecting tissue of ideas being that ancient half-science and half-art known as physiognomy.

How classical humoralism and physiognomical theories about the "sympathy" between mental and physical features lingered on in the Victorian era can best be seen in the antithesis of those two familiar stereotypes, prognathous Paddy and orthognathous Anglo-Saxon, which are found in the cartoons of John Leech, John Tenniel, Matt Morgan, Harry Furniss, and John Proctor in London, and Thomas Nast, Joseph Keppler, and James A. Wales in New York. In marked contrast to these "Anglo-Saxonist" stereotypes, the cartoonists of Dublin, in particular such ardent Home Rulers as John Fergus O'Hea, Thomas Fitzpatrick, John D. Reigh, and W. T. O'Shea, completely reversed the stereotypes made in London and New York. These men turned Paddy the prognathous and simian peasant into Pat the honest farmer, a man of noble features as well as behavior. In Irish nationalist cartoons, the agents of British rule in Ireland—including the constabulary, bailiffs, informers, Orangemen, and John Bull himself—were turned into brutes with huge mouths and heavy jaws. On occasion, a Dublin cartoonist would single out an English cartoon denigrating Irish character and then produce a devastating parody for Home Rule consumption. Dublin's cartoonists, in short, not only kept an eye on the productions of their analogues in London, but worked hard to counter the "Anglo-Saxonist" image of the simianized political agitator in Ireland.

In a short study of this kind it would be absurd to pretend that one had "exhausted" a subject so rich in human comedy and so full of chromatic fantasies. This inquiry covers only a small patch of a field which might be called historical physiognomy, and historians who think that this field can be easily surveyed and fenced off are in for a surprise. There is no discussion here of Irish faces in portraiture and in illustrated editions of Irish novels and folktales. No more than half the comic periodicals which were launched in London, Dublin, and New York between 1840 and 1900 have been mentioned. Countless questions remain unanswered, in some cases for want of adequate documentation. It would help, for example, to know much more about the finances, management, and circulation of the comic weeklies and monthlies. More information is needed about their readers—who they were, where they came from, and how they reacted to the comic ingredients. Biographical details about the cartoonists immediately below the rank or stature of Tenniel, Furniss, and Nast are exceedingly scarce and not always reliable. One would like to know more about the training and the working methods of the comic artists, not to mention their financial condition, which remains virtually unexplored. As the questions increase and multiply, the few available answers begin to dissolve into conjecture. The once popular, now neglected, world of comic art, including the copywriters and the less famous artists, many of whom died in obscurity, cries out for serious and sympathetic investigation.

Much of the raw material for this study belongs to a world not only colloquial and "lowbrow," but elusive. One has to probe behind the manifest comic content of cartoons in order to grasp the serious implications of this medium. The study of comic art, especially in its more political guise, can be an enriching experience, forcing the inquirer into fields far removed from his point of departure. But the subject has its frustrations, if only because so much of the evidence about motives, effects, and affects is either fragmentary or fleeting. Victorian political cartoons were closely linked to popular prejudices about all manner of people and issues. Here and there, those prejudices can be traced directly from the cartoons back to that vast subterranean culture—unwritten and full of slang—which has no place in our respectable history books. The simianization of Irish "rebels" in the nineteenth century was not entirely confined to the comic weeklies. If we are to believe one tantalizing allusion by the Anglo-Irish novelist, Edith Somerville, the gentry of Ireland also indulged in the ape-like metaphor and the simian simile. The opening page of her novel about the decline and fall of a once proud Anglo-Irish family, entitled *The Big House of Inver*, con-contains the following clue:

> . . . high on Ross Inver stood the tower, tall and square, that, since the time of his Norman ancestor who built it, had guarded the Prendevilles from those whom they and their companion adventurers called, with soldierly arrogance, The Wild Irish—as who, in later days, should say The Gorillas.

More than a hint, but less than an irrefutable piece of evidence with which to prove that Anglo-Irish landowners shared the same compulsions as those comic artists who turned Paddy into a gorilla with a few deft strokes of the pen. Allusions to Irish ape-men are not often found in the diaries and letters of the Anglo-Irish gentry. Only in Victorian political cartoons, designed to amuse the ruling classes on both sides of the Irish Sea, do we find the equation clearly and repeatedly stated that anthropoid apes and Irish Fenians had much in common.

Men have used apes and monkeys for seemly and unseemly comparisons with themselves since time immemorial, and homologous studies of the higher primates for both scientific and fantastic ("Planet of the Apes") purposes show no signs of abating at the present time. Man's fascination with apes has been almost as intense as his obsession with angels, whose company he has usually preferred to that of his hairier relations in the Pongidae family. In Pope's *Essay on Man* there is a forceful reminder about the price men pay for their lofty aspirations:

> Men would be angels, angels would be gods.
> Aspiring to be gods if angels fell,
> Aspiring to be angels men rebel.

There were many kinds of rebellion in Victorian politics and society, few of which came close to success. One of the most impressive rebellions, however, took place in the minds of respectable men and women who, "aspiring to be angels," refused to accept the theory that their nearest ancestors were anthropoid apes.

Caricature is, by definition, a distortion of reality; and so too is the stereotype. Caricaturists and those who called themselves cartoonists in Victorian times are supposed to differ from men of ordinary abilities and prejudices in that they set out quite deliberately to distort reality in order to achieve a particular comic or satirical effect. This is not to say that Victorian comic artists had no prejudices. During and after the 1860s many cartoonists seemed anxious to make some men look like apes who had recently descended from the trees, while depicting other men as angels, who may once have fallen from a state of grace but who had nevertheless been created in the image of God. Who belonged to which category and why these artists placed them there constitute the main themes of this "mono(litho)graph."

Acknowledgments

THIS STUDY is a revised and expanded version of a paper entitled "Apes, Angels, and Irishmen: A Study in Victorian Physiognomy," which was read at the conference of the American Committee for Irish Studies, held at Cortland, New York, on 10 May 1968. During the revision stage the title, like the subject matter, evolved by a process of more or less natural selection, replete with certain residual ethnic sensitivities, into the present one. In spite of this adaptation, the title still owes much to the inspiration of the late William Irvine's book, *Apes, Angels, and Victorians* (New York: McGraw-Hill Book Company, Inc., 1955).

The author would like to thank not only those who offered comments at the conference at Cortland, but also Professor Roger Hahn of the University of California at Berkeley, who read an earlier draft and gave valuable advice; Dr. Carl Seltzer of Harvard University, who supplied both encouragement and guidance through the thickets of modern physical anthropology; the staff of the National Library of Ireland, in particular Mr. James Scully and Mr. Michael Hewson, who dredged up countless examples of Irish comic art with unfailing good humor; and Mr. Brendan MacGiolla Choille, Keeper of State Papers, Dublin Castle, whose knowledge of the Fenians and the Fenian Papers in his keeping is unrivaled. Lastly, thanks are due to Miss Louise Heskett, whose editorial skill and imagination have sustained this volume throughout.

CHAPTER I

Physiognomy:
Ancient and Modern

IN THE YEAR 1880 Gustave de Molinari (1819–1912), the Belgian political economist and radical essayist, published a series of epistolary articles on the condition of Ireland in the *Journal des Débats*. Molinari's survey of the Irish scene may not have equaled Gustave de Beaumont's notable inquiry of the 1830s in breadth of knowledge and depth of insight, but there was one passage in his appraisal of Anglo-Irish relations which shows him to have been a perceptive observer of social and political realities. England's largest newspapers, he wrote, "allow no occasion to escape them of treating the Irish as an inferior race—as a kind of white negroes [sic]—and a glance at *Punch* is sufficient to show the difference they establish between the plump and robust personification of John Bull and the wretched figure of lean and bony Pat."[1]

Molinari deserves credit for having spotted one of the more widespread images of the Irish which was entertained by educated and respectable Victorians who habitually thought in categorical terms about the so-called races of man. The allusion to "white negroes" points up a vital ingredient in the cluster of prejudices which operated so pervasively in Great Britain against not only Irishmen but Negroes and other non-Anglo-Saxons whose assumed inferiority was even less open to dispute or qualification. These prejudices were continually being reinforced by a number of assumptions and axioms about the physical and mental traits of mankind. In the case of the Irish there were many slurs and aspersions on the tips of British tongues in the Victorian era, all of which reflected the conviction that Englishmen and Irishmen were separated from one another by irreconcilable differences not only of religion and culture but, above all, of temperament.

There was, of course, more than one image of the Irish competing for a place in the minds of Victorians, and not all of those images were as derogatory as Molinari contended. Those who cherished either positive or negative images were usually shrewd enough to concede the existence of more than one type of Irishman. But it would be quite incorrect to assume that the category of "white Negroes" was the lowest possible common denominator into which the Irish Celt could be placed. The student of Anglo-Irish relations in the nineteenth century is bound to encounter sooner or later enough evidence to establish that the fall of the stereotypical Irishman from a state of disgrace in Anglo-Saxon eyes took him farther down the scale of mankind or, rather, the Hominoidea, so that by the 1860s the "repre-

1

sentative Irishman" was to all appearances an anthropoid ape. Among the forces that accelerated Paddy's degeneration was the assumption that there were qualities in Irish Celts which marked them off as a race or breed quite distinct in looks and behavior from those who claimed Anglo-Saxon, Danish, or Norman ancestry in the British Isles. Granting that there were indeed *some* noticeable differences between Englishmen and Irishmen in terms of behavior and physical features, those differences were not sufficient in themselves to explain the belief of so many Victorians that the physical and mental traits of Irish Celts and Anglo-Saxons were not only profoundly antithetical, but also could not be altered except through massive miscegenation.

If educated Victorians—and by Victorians we do not mean just the English upper middle classes—had done no more than construct mutually derogatory comparisons between Irishmen and the Chinese, Hottentots, Maoris, Aborigines, Sudanese, and other "barbarians," life might have been a shade less harsh for the vast majority of Irish Catholics.[2] But some Victorians on both sides of the Atlantic went further by discovering features in Irish character which they took to be completely simian or anthropoid. In cartoons and caricatures as well as in prose, Paddy began to resemble increasingly the chimpanzee, the orangutan, and, finally, the gorilla. The transformation of peasant Paddy into an ape-man or simianized Caliban was completed by the 1860s and 1870s, when for various reasons it became necessary for a number of Victorians to assign Irishmen to a place closer to the apes than the angels. How and why the feckless, amusing, bibulous, and apolitical stage-Irishman or Teague of an earlier epoch evolved into the distinctly dangerous ape-man of the later nineteenth century constitutes the central theme of this study.

The study of images, that is, those relatively inflexible impressions which some people entertain at all times about other people, can be approached from many avenues. The actual choice of direction depends on what kinds of evidence appear to yield the most valuable information about both the image itself and the reasons why that particular image was so attractive to the holder. Virtually all images are sustained by a conglomeration of value judgments, usually expressed in adjectival form, about the apparent mental and physical traits of the group in question. Without this array of ascribed features most images would simply sink or dissolve in a sea of vague impressions. In order to understand Victorian images of the Irish, a task which includes Irish images of the English as well as of themselves, we must look first at the combination of physical and mental traits which were most often assigned to that singular category known as Paddy. Instead of trying to compile an annual register of English, Scottish, and Irish images of each other, drawn from such sources as newspapers, pamphlets, diaries, and letters, the present study is confined to the nature and meaning of those physiognomical features which Victorians were so fond of applying to whole regions and countries. Only by probing into what might be called the popular scientific lore of the Victorian age can we begin to appreciate the full significance of Paddy's degeneration into a rather hairy ape-man.

Because physical appearances in general and facial features in particular form an indispensable part of every national, racial, ethnic, social, and sexual stereotype, we must venture back beyond the descriptions of Irishmen in the nineteenth century to classical antiquity, when some of the theories about human nature and behavior with which we are concerned first made their appearance in written form. Recognizability of the type or group in question constitutes a necessary part of the stereotyping process, and no stereotype is complete unless it possesses a more or less unique set of features. The attribution of physical and mental traits to any given type of man belongs to what used to be called physiognomy, a branch of the science of man which may well be as old as man himself. Neither entirely clinical nor occult in its so-called methods, and by no means confined to any particular country or culture, physiognomy may be construed as the art cum science of judging character and temperament from the features of the head and face, the body, and the extremities. Physiognomy has always had a strong appeal to those people who seek a simple and painless way of assessing their fellow human beings without having to resort to astrology, palmistry, or medical examination.[3]

At first sight the theory and practice of physiognomy may seem to have little connection with Victorian images of the Irish, but then first sights, whether of ideas or faces, can be notoriously misleading. Victorian novels, for example, abound with passages which depict the facial features and stature of the principal characters. Examples of this long-established literary habit may be found in a variety of works ranging from Sir Walter Scott and Lord Lytton to Charles Kingsley, Dickens, Trollope, Disraeli, and Kipling. All of these writers sought to inform their readers about the characters and personalities of their protagonists by means of brief but vivid descriptions of their physical traits. In many cases ethnicity, or the patterns of behavior assigned by Victorians to men of Saxon, Danish, Norman, or Celtic ancestry, also figured in these physiognomical sketches. A good example of the technique may be found in W. Steuart Trench's romantic historical novel, *Ierne, A Tale*, wherein the hero, Donald O'Sulevan Beare, is introduced in the following manner:

> His nose was more Grecian than aquiline, a well formed compromise between the upturned nostril of the Celt and the Norman tendency to the eagle's beak; whilst his short upper lip and expressive mouth seemed to portray a temperament unusually quick.[4]

Donald's beautiful young sister, Ierne, receives much the same kind of physiognomical treatment:

> Her stature was tall. Her appearance was very singular, and she seemed to partake of qualities belonging both to Saxon and Celt. Her hair was

3

auburn. . . . But though her hair was Saxon, her eyes were purely Celt, large, dark, and rich; and the contrast between her chestnut hair and dark eyes, eyelashes and eyebrows was very striking. Her nose was Grecian, and her upper lips short and expressive.[5]

The physiognomical device was used by Charles Dickens when he portrayed Thomas Gradgrind in *Hard Times*:

The emphasis was helped by the speaker's square wall of a forehead, which had his eyebrows for a base, while his eyes found commodious cellarage in two dark caves, overshadowed by the wall. The emphasis was helped by the speaker's mouth, which was wide, thin, and hard set. The emphasis was helped by the speaker's voice, which was inflexible, dry, and dictatorial.[6]

Who was "Phiz" (Hablot K. Browne), the famous illustrator of Dickens' works, if not a gifted physiognomist? Physiognomical observations abound in *The Adventures and Memoirs of Sherlock Holmes*. A. Conan Doyle was, of course, a doctor who had been trained at Edinburgh to observe the minutest features of both cadavers and patients. Perhaps the best known example of this device in criminal fiction is Professor Moriarty's remark upon meeting Holmes for the first time at 221 Baker Street: "You have less frontal development than I should have expected."[7] Novelists still use the principles of physiognomy in order to convey to their readers the essence of a character's personality before the plot or story has progressed far enough to reveal his real nature. Such obvious features as color of hair and eyes, complexion, shape and size of forehead, nose, mouth, ears, and lower jaw, especially the chin, are used as a form of code by novelists, not to mention other kinds of men and women, to reveal the inner being of the person being described.

One final example of the physiognomical device in literature deserves to be quoted at this point, because it illuminates several facets of the problem that concern us. Mat Brady, the villain of Emily Lawless's haunting novel about rural life in the Burren country of County Clare, *Hurrish, A Study*, is first encountered by the reader behaving like a lecher toward the purest girl for miles around:

After her in full pursuit followed a man—unwieldy, red-faced, heavy-jawed, brutal—a sort of human orang-outang or Caliban, whose lumbering action and coarse gesture had something grotesque and even repulsive about them, as [if] it were a parody or perversion of humanity.[8]

Later on, Brady fails in his attempt to shoot the hero, Hurrish O'Brien, who flushes the villain from his hiding place and closes in for what turns out to be the unintentional kill:

Then, like a beast, he [Brady] turned at bay, and like a beast's was the face which presented itself,—the lowering brow, the huge jaw, the mouth distorted and gnashing with rage and terror! A hideous sight—to dream of, not to tell—a man in the likeness of a beast, worse than the very ugliest variety with hoofs or claws.[9]

4

Emily Lawless was not only of impeccable Anglo-Irish stock, being the daughter of Lord Cloncurry, but a woman in love with the Celtic soul of Ireland; and the virtuous, noble Irish peasants of her story were all endowed with features far removed from those of "the great red-headed, half-tipsy Caliban" who met his just fate beneath Hurrish's shillelagh.

The assumption that physical features and mental or emotional states are bound together in the same physiological system is an ancient one, and the once reputable science of physiognomy boasts a past littered with weighty treatises and discourses dealing with the interaction of physical and mental traits in both animals and man. Although regarded for centuries as that branch of science dealing with the diagnosis and cure of disease or organic disorders, classical physiognomy also involved a certain amount of divination and fortune-telling. For those who wish to believe that the face never lies, that the eyes are windows into the mind or soul, and that the color of hair and eyes or the shape of the nose and mouth reveal temperament, physiognomy was and is the answer. By the early 1800s physiognomical dogma had become part of the popular scientific folklore, and men from all walks of life in every part of Europe relied to some degree on this method of "seeing through" their neighbors as well as strangers from other lands.

This is not the place to recapitulate all the varieties and vagaries of physiognomical lore from ancient to modern times, but a brief summary of the main body of thought may serve to place Victorian images of the Irish and other peoples in their proper context. Physiognomy was, indeed, an international phenomenon, with its most renowned students and practitioners coming not only from ancient Greece and Rome but also from France, Spain, Italy, Germany, and England during the Enlightenment. Educated men and women all over Europe, not to mention other continents, accepted this body of scientific lore as the next best thing to gospel. Just as physiognomical theories traversed national frontiers, so they crossed class lines within each of those countries, and entered every level of education from elementary schools to universities. Physiognomical convictions could be found among the most educated and prosperous families as well as among those members of the working classes who believed in "the evil eye" or dreaded meeting strangers with red hair on the road. In Victorian England some of the most ardent exponents of this theory were those university-educated or self-taught men, mostly medical doctors, clergymen, antiquarians, natural scientists with a modest private income, minor civil servants, and army officers, who called themselves ethnologists and anthropologists.

In ancient Greece, physiognomy formed a branch of physiology and was considered an indispensable method of detecting organic as well as emotional disorders in people. According to the Hippocratic school of physiology, facial features provided infallible clues to the somatic and pneumatic or life-giving qualities of mankind. Even a cursory examination of skin, hair,

5

and eyes, and size and shape of face was sufficient to reveal the nature of the humors and pneuma which determined health and behavior. In the Hippocratic schema the four moist humors of blood, phlegm, black and yellow bile—which corresponded to the four basic elements of fire, water, earth, and air—were supposed to exist in harmonious balance within every healthy body; and this simple geometrical pattern provided men of science and the healing arts with an authoritative basis for dividing mankind into the sanguine, phlegmatic, melancholic, and choleric types.[10] The essay *On Physiognomy* attributed to Aristotle served to reinforce Hippocratic physiognomy. This influential treatise explained how facial features, complexion, color and texture of hair, as well as voice and posture revealed not only the "natural passions of the soul," but human affinities with animals as well. These physical features provided a way of ascertaining the extent of a man's fortitude or timidity, good nature or irascibility, impudence or torpor, and so forth. The Aristotelian assumption that "the soul and body sympathize with each other" underlies all subsequent theories of physiognomy. Aristotle's ideal man possessed symmetrical, harmonious features matched by an equally balanced temperament made up of the right proportions of all four humors.[11] Neither too sanguine nor melancholy, neither too phlegmatic nor choleric, neither too hairy nor hairless, neither fat nor thin, this Aristotelian archetype survived more or less intact into the Victorian period, when it became the model of the manly, respectable, and self-controlled English gentleman so highly prized among the governing and educated classes. Hippocratic and Aristotelian physiognomy was reinforced as well as revised in the second century A.D. by Galen whose synthetic physiological system combined aspects of Hippocratic humoralism with newer views about the role of the pneuma in causing disease and abnormal behavior.

Although diffuse in theory, deficient in method, and subjective in practice, physiognomy remained a relatively coherent and definitely popular body of beliefs and axioms for the next thousand years. In spite of revisionist disputes and satirical attacks, the basic faith of physiognomists in the symbiotic relationship of physical and mental traits lived on, proving itself highly resistant to that inexorable and often mysterious process which textbook writers have called "the rise of modern science." Neither Vesalius's contributions to anatomy nor Harvey's discovery of the constant circulation of the blood succeeded in driving out the baser coinage of popular physiognomy with its humoral bias. Many Europeans and Englishmen continued to prefer a less clinical and more simplistic approach to human behavior and character, although some began to eschew the descriptive method of the Aristotelian school for a more anatomical and physiological perspective. Regardless of the method espoused, most physiognomists continued to insist that the salient features of the head and face revealed the character of the individual as well as the type to which he belonged. To the informed observer the face was like an elaborate contour map which could be read at a glance. Every physiognomist had his favorite feature which served as a kind of skeleton key to unlock the secrets of human motivation and behavior, some preferring the forehead, others the nose, eyes, ears, mouth, and so on.

No discussion of physiognomy in the modern period would be anything less than hollow without some passing reference to the work of Johann Kaspar Lavater (1741–1801), Pieter Camper (1722–89), Johann Friedrich Blumenbach (1752–1840), Sir Charles Bell (1774–1842), and James C. Prichard (1786–1848). Lavater was a Zurich-born cosmopolite and minister who had no formal training in anatomy or physiology. His first essay on physiognomy appeared in 1772 heralding almost thirty years of investigation of this subject. In the best tradition of philosophic rationalism, Lavater compiled his famous *Physiognomical Fragments* "for the Promotion of the Knowledge and Love of Mankind," but his analysis of faces and character proved that he was more of an impressionist and intuitionist than a rationalist in practice.[12] The Lavaterian method, such as it was, consisted of a close scrutiny of the features of head and face followed by an attempt to define the character of each in terms supposedly more precise than his predecessors. A universalist by nature, Lavater tried to incorporate the countenances of animals as well as humans into his system. He surveyed the noses, eyes, mouths, and lower jaws of nations, races, regions, towns, families, and individuals with equal confidence in his own judgment. Despite criticism of both his emphasis on the facial features and neglect of the emotions and their expression, Lavater won a commanding place among the physiognomists of the world, and royalty as well as other leading dignitaries visited him in Zurich in order to have their characters read.

Lavater's prolific writings spurred physiognomical investigations all over Europe, including Holland, where Pieter Camper combined both art and science in order to differentiate higher from lower forms of vertebrate life. What caused Camper no little concern was the width of the gap which separated the races of man from the quadrumana and other animals. Camper solved the problem to his own satisfaction by devising the facial angle or line which was supposed to mark clear distinctions between the skulls—and therefore the intelligence—of monkeys, orangutans, Negroes, Kalmucks, and Europeans. The facial angle was formed by the intersection of two lines, one running diagonally or vertically, as the case might be, from the forehead to the foremost point of the front teeth or incisors, and the other running horizontally from the opening of the ear to the nostrils.[13] This relatively, if not alarmingly, simple device permitted Camper to contrive a scale of animal and human evolution or progress from primitive to civilized life, the intervals between each stage being gauged by the size of the facial angle in each category. Although he did not popularize the terms orthognathism and prognathism, Camper reinforced the notion that the position of the lower jaw and mouth in relation to the upper portion of the face and skull was the decisive criterion of organic development from primitivism to civilization.

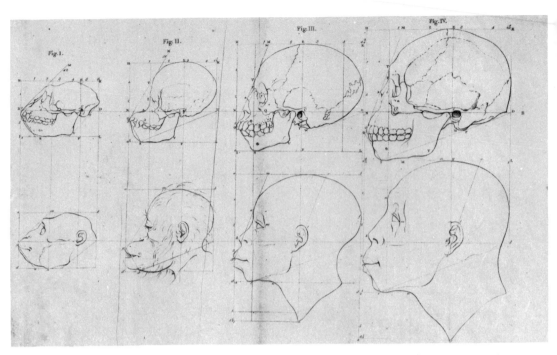

1 *Camper's Facial Angles.* Pieter Camper's facial angle is illustrated by the profiles and skulls in his own collection. The angles read from left to right: I, tailed monkey, 42°; II, orangutan, 58°; III, Negro, 70°; and IV, Kalmuck, 70°. (From T. Cogan, editor, *The Works of the Late Professor Camper on the Connection between the Science of Anatomy and the Arts of Drawing, Painting, Statuary.* London, 1821.)

The facial angle of his tailed monkey's skull measured 42°, that of his orangutan 58°, compared with the skull of a young Negro at 70°, and that of a Kalmuck also at 70°. Camper then compared these figures with the facial angle of his European skull—a selective sample of one, needless to say—which measured 80°. The angles of his Grecian and Roman busts ranged from an ideal 90° to 95°. Camper concluded from his survey of cranial types that the normal, that is to say, desirable, facial angle for European men lay between 70° and 80°. Any angle less than this was by definition a sign of barbarism or more primitive life, and anything higher than 80° belonged to the realm of wishful thinking or to that of diseases like hydrocephalus.[14]
   Although the distinguished naturalist and anthropologist of Göttingen, Johann Friedrich Blumenbach, disputed the validity of Camper's facial angle, his own treatise on comparative anatomy and human variety played a part in perpetuating certain myths about the races of man. This relatively cautious and critical scientist questioned the notion that Negroes were inherently and permanently inferior to Caucasians and other primary races in terms of potential intelligence, and his reasons for rejecting Camper's angle still carry conviction.[15] His fivefold division of the races of man into the

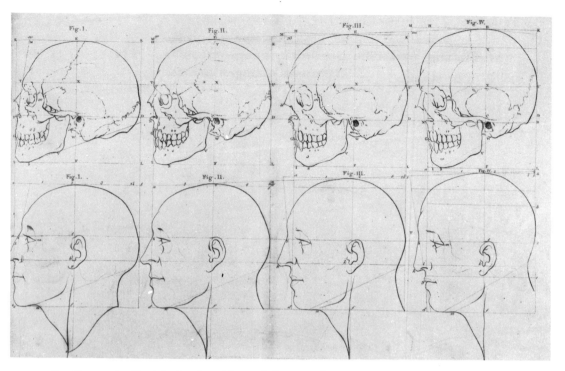

2 *Camper's Facial Angles.* From left to right: I, European, 80°; II, Grecian bust, 90°; III, Roman bust, 95°; and IV, a case of hydrocephalus, 100°. (From T. Cogan, editor, *The Works of the Late Professor Camper on the Connection between the Science of Anatomy and the Arts of Drawing, Painting, Statuary.* London, 1821.)

Caucasian, Mongol, Malay, Ethiopian, and American groups was eventually adopted by many anthropologists. Blumenbach was a staunch monogenist who believed that all the nonwhite races were essentially degenerations from the original Caucasian stock. His emphasis upon the morphological differences between the white and nonwhite races, however, did little to discourage the notion, so appealing to Europeans, that it was better to be a Caucasian than a member of any other race.[16]

Another important contributor to the art cum science of physiognomy was Sir Charles Bell, the distinguished Edinburgh surgeon and student of the nervous system, who published an important treatise in 1806 entitled *Essays on the Anatomy of Expression in Painting.*[17] Like both Lavater and Camper, Bell was also an artist. Unlike them, however, he was a student of pathognomy, and he turned his attention to the operation of the muscles and nerves which conveyed changing emotions to the surface of the face. Like any good surgeon-artist, Bell took pains to analyze and then draw the range of human emotions from love and hate to laughter and madness. Pathognomy, or the study of the passions and emotions as expressed in the face, did not end with Bell. His work won the respect of Charles Darwin, whose *The Expression of the Emotions in Man and Animals*, published in 1872, carried forward this investigation by closer comparison of facial expressions in men and animals. Darwin explicitly denied any concern with physiognomy, but his work overlapped that of Lavater and Camper as well as Bell at several points.[18]

Not the least remarkable feature of physiognomy was the way it spilled over into other fields and disciplines associated with human behavior. Many working anthropologists, ethnologists, craniologists, zoologists, and medical doctors relied unwittingly or otherwise on physiognomical assumptions in their efforts to classify the races and subraces of man. If the more prognostic and divinatory dimension of physiognomy fell by the scientific wayside, the belief in the intimate connection of physical and mental traits did not suffer from undernourishment. A good example of the persistence of that belief may be found in James Cowles Prichard's *Researches into the Physical History of Man*, published in London in 1813.[19] In his spirited defense of the monogenist thesis that all the races of man descended from a single act of creation or pair of parents, Prichard accounted for the external physical differences among men as proof of the "natural law of diversification." Convinced of the "specific unity" of man, he sought to reconcile the variety of pigmental and facial features in man with scripture in order to refute the polygenist school once and for all. Prichard was an unabashed physiognomist who insisted that physical features revealed not only ethnicity and ancestry, but character and temperament. His division of Europeans into the four familiar categories of the sanguine, phlegmatic, melancholic, and choleric types, based on color of skin, hair, and eyes, illustrated the extent of his borrowing from the Hippocratic and Aristotelian schools.

According to Prichard's classification, the sanguine type was marked by reddish hair, blue eyes, and a ruddy complexion. The temperament accompanying these features was not only "acute" but emotional, hedonistic, and somewhat irritable. The phlegmatic man had light or sandy hair, light grey eyes, and a pallid complexion. Owing to weak blood circulation, this type suffered from torpor and muscular inactivity and tended to be deficient in cheerfulness and vitality as well as "dull and insensible." The choleric man had black curly hair, dark eyes, a swarthy complexion, and a "thick rough hairy skin." Closer in some respects to the sanguine type, he was strong-minded and more easily angered than men of lighter hue. The melancholic type also had black or dark hair and eyes and a dark complexion, but his hair was lanky, his skin yellowish, and his pulse slow. He suffered from torpor of the nervous system and weak blood circulation and was therefore highly susceptible to insanity and other kinds of mental disorder.[20] Prichard's taxonomy did not go unchallenged during the next few decades, but his conviction that skin color and facial features corresponded with the four humors and explained character or mental traits was repeated by more than one prominent anthropologist as late as 1885.[21] The interdependence of pigment, complexion, and facial features on the one hand, and national and racial character on the other was regarded as axiomatic by most members of the anthropological and ethnological societies in Victorian England as well as by their analogues on the continent, and in a more generalized form this physiognomical belief was shared by Victorians from all walks of life and regions of the British Isles.

The work of Anders Adolf Retzius (1796–1860), the Swedish ethnologist and craniologist, provides another example of the ubiquity of physiognomical lore. Although not a physiognomist in any formal sense, and having more in common with English craniologists like J. Barnard Davis and J. Thurnam than with Lavater or Camper, Retzius sought to differentiate the races of man on the basis of skull types. Retzius's international reputation owed less to his comparative analysis of Swedish and Finnish skulls than to his reliance on a new index to distinguish the races of man. By means of the cephalic index, or ratio of the maximum breadth and length of the cranium, he divided mankind into two main categories, the dolichocephalics or long-heads and the brachycephalics or roundheads. The cephalic index became one of the standard gauges used by ethnologists and craniometrists around the world.[22] Retzius also attached much significance to prognathous and orthognathous features, a concern that recalled Camper's facial angle owing to the assumptions underlying this criterion. This emphasis on prognathism seemed to confirm old beliefs that a protruding jaw and receding forehead in man indicated mental as well as physical similarities with anthropoid apes. The application of calipers and measuring tapes to skulls after the early 1840s gave many scientists of man a new sense of confidence in the precision of their methods, even though craniologists could not effectively distinguish between male and female skulls in practice. For all their wealth of data, these men usually began and ended their craniological studies on the premise that some frontal, parietal, occipital, and zygomatic developments were morally, intellectually, and aesthetically better than others. The old equation between size of cranial cavity or brain and intelligence thus lived on in the best craniometrical circles.

Physiognomy also permeated such newer disciplines as phrenology and criminal anthropology. Phrenology, defined as the science of mental faculties as revealed by examining the external form of the skull, became a fashionable cult in Europe and America after 1815, largely on the strength of its three forceful apostles, F. J. Gall, J. K. Spurzheim, and G. Combe. In some respects, the high priests of phrenology were latter day physiognomists, armed with an impressive vocabulary and a technique designed to reveal mental traits. This was merely divination by another name. In the middle decades of the century, phrenologists filled public lecture halls and their consulting rooms with rapt believers, including Richard Cobden and George Eliot, bent on having their heads examined for a modest fee. Phrenology had the advantage over physiognomy of dynamic leadership and an apparently authentic map of the mental faculties in the brain. The laying on of hands by phrenologists, whose fingers probed for cranial declivities and protrusions indicating the degree of such things as amativeness, philoprogenitiveness, and combativeness, must have had a therapeutic function also. From Edinburgh the *Phrenological Journal* (1824–47) spread the gospel of Gall and Spurzheim among the faithful and the curious, and its pages were filled with "phrenoscopes" or analyses of famous heads, past and present.[23]

Fragments of physiognomy also found their way into criminal anthropology during the 1870s and 1880s. Physiognomists had always been interested in detecting violent and criminal tendencies in the face, and Francis Galton's efforts in the 1870s and after to devise a taxonomy of human types by means of anthropometric and psychometric tests—not to mention his technique of composite photography—led him directly to the study of criminals. Galton's composite pictures of murderers and thieves, as well as Jewish and phthisic or tubercular types, contained the implicit, if not explicit, statement that the face was indeed a mirror of the criminal, ethnic, or pathological interior of every man. The net effect of Galton's researches into "human faculty" and the laws of transmission of mental traits was to suggest that men were born criminals, geniuses, officers, rankers, or inherently superior and inferior, and that there was little they could do to change their lot.[24] Galton's work on composite stereotypes impressed the greatest of late-nineteenth-century criminal anthropologists, Cesare Lombroso (1836–1909), whose classic study, *L'Uomo delinquente*, published in 1876, and other writings represented a hodgepodge of sociology, psychology, penology, physical anthropology, and physiognomy, as well as a good measure of wishful thinking.[25] Lombroso was to modern criminology what Blumenbach was to modern anthropology, and his investigation of the etiology of political as well as social crime, including the backgrounds of rebels and revolutionaries, had a marked impact on many contemporaries, not to mention devoted disciples like Gustav Aschaffenberg in Germany.[26]

Like most branches of science, physiognomy spawned some extravagant treatises that made Lavater's work look systematic and objective. James W. Redfield's *Comparative Physiognomy*, published in 1852, pushed the frontiers of physiognomy beyond Lavater by likening Prussians to cats, Negroes to elephants and fish, Englishmen to bulls, Turks to turkeys, Chinese to hogs, Americans to bears, Russians to geese, and Irish to dogs. In fact, he equated proverbial "Irish eloquence" with the barking of dogs. He wrote:

> Compare the Irishman and the dog in respect to barking, snarling, howling, begging, fawning, flattering, backbiting, quarrelling, blustering, scenting, seizing, hanging on, teasing, rollicking, and whatever other traits you may discover in either, and you will be convinced that there is a wonderful resemblance.[27]

After dwelling on the Irishman's capacity for enjoying both pleasure and pain and his love of intoxication, Redfield drew a sharp distinction between the genuine Irishman of Ireland, resembling the noble Irish wolfhound and St. Bernard, and the noisy Irish immigrant in America and elsewhere, who was more like "a scavenger-dog of the city and the great variety of whining, barking, howling, snarling, snapping dogs. . . ."[28]

Two Americans by the names of Samuel and Anna Cherry, with a fetish for ears, wrote a book called *Otyognomy, Or the External Ear as an Index to Character*, which was published in 1900. Another savant in England adopted noses as the key to personality and discussed Greek, Roman, Jewish, cogitative, and other nasal varieties in his *Nasology* (1848).[29] But these diverting variations on the Lavaterian theme should not be allowed to obscure such relatively sober works as G. B. A. Duchenne's *Mécanisme de la Physionomie humaine* (1862), L. P. Gratiolet's *De la Physionomie et des Mouvements d'Expression* (1865), Paolo Mantegazza's *Physiognomy and Expression* (1890),[30] and Paul Hartenberg's *Physionomie et Caractère* (1908).

In spite of numerous advances in anatomy, physiology, and medical pathology since the time of Galen, the assortment of ideas, assumptions, axioms, and fantasies which may be subsumed under the heading of physiognomy still influenced many well-educated scientists and laymen in the nineteenth century. If men trained at the best medical schools in Europe as well as in London and Edinburgh imbibed large doses of physiognomy from their teachers of anatomy and physiology, and if doctors continued to rely on facial features to provide clues not just to disease—which at times made good clinical sense—but also to character, imagine how widespread these beliefs were among the public at large. Indeed, some of the truest believers in the remnants of classical physiognomy were found in the anthropological and ethnological societies of London where they presented papers saturated with physiognomical data and speculations about the races of man. The leading members of these societies, men like James Hunt and John Crawfurd, had a habit of extolling Caucasians with features like their own, while pointing out the inherent, even permanent, shortcomings of those with contrasting facial and pigmental features. The advent of increasingly quantitative and ethnocentric forms of physical anthropology helped to provide many middle- and upper-middle-class Victorians with scientific justification for believing that they stood at the very top of the tree representing the races of man. The bottom limbs of that tree were occupied by such groups as Hottentots, Negritos, African Bushmen, and Australian Aborigines.[31]

Whether seen from a scientific, social, or cultural perspective, the Victorian images of the Irish as "white Negro" and simian Celt, or a combination of the two, derived much of its force and inspiration from physiognomical beliefs. But this image was not just an indigenous artifact produced by and for Englishmen alone. Virtually every country in Europe had its equivalent of "white Negroes" and simianized men, whether or not they happened to be stereotypes of criminals, assassins, political radicals, revolutionaries,

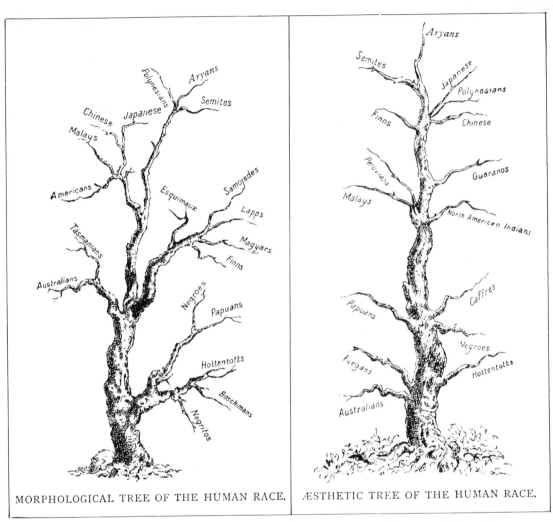

MORPHOLOGICAL TREE OF THE HUMAN RACE. | ÆSTHETIC TREE OF THE HUMAN RACE.

3 *Mantegazza's Taxonomy of Races.* Paolo Mantegazza illustrated his notions about the morphological and aesthetic value or rank of the races of man by using this arboreal device. His "intellectual tree," not illustrated here, ranked the Aryans and Semites as equals at the top of the tree. (From Paolo Mantegazza, *Physiognomy and Expression*, plates 2 and 4, pages 312 and 314. London, 1904 edition.)

Slavs, gypsies, Jews, or peasants. This Victorian image of the Irish was in fact only one product of a polygonal prism of images which refracted much the same light in as many different directions as there were outgroups for Europeans and Englishmen to worry about. No matter if the people or races being measured and physiognomized lived in Europe, Africa, Asia, or America, the refracted image worked in the same way to enhance the self-esteem of the beholder at the expense of those being stereotyped. European and British anthropologists, many of them with the best of monogenistic

14

intentions, gave their scientific authority to these images and stereotypes simply because they subscribed unquestioningly to the orthodox ethnocentrism of their day, class, and country.

Reasons of space prevent anything more than a passing allusion to two other sources of anti-Irish prejudice in England which reinforced this ethnocentric outlook. These were religious and class prejudices as they operated in the minds of middle- and upper-class Victorian Protestants against lower-class Irish Roman Catholics. Since these prejudices are discussed in more detail below, it need only be mentioned here that for most Englishmen the word "Irishman" usually evoked such loaded terms as Papists and peasants. Since prejudices based upon marked differences of religion and social class had flourished so long in English and Scottish minds where Catholic Irishmen were concerned, it was all the easier for some Victorians to conclude that the relative paucity among Irishmen of skilled workers and professional men proved beyond all doubt that the Irish were an inferior people incapable of self-help and therefore unfit to govern themselves through Anglo-Saxon institutions.

If educated and responsible Victorians had formed such unfavorable impressions of Irish Celtic character, their images of Negroes and other non-white peoples were even less flattering; and Irishmen could at least console themselves with the fact that they occupied a rung on most, although not all, of the English-made ladders of racial development somewhat above their African cousins. But what concerns us here is not the entire prism of English images of other peoples, but the way in which the science of man and the art of caricature—working both independently of one another and at times together—helped to harden as well as perpetuate the stereotypes of "white Negroes" and simianized Celts.

CHAPTER II   # The Ethnology of Irish Celts

THROUGHOUT THE VICTORIAN ERA a small and influential group of gentlemen, including antiquarians, historians, doctors, barristers, and clergymen took part in the quest for the racial origins of the modern inhabitants of the British Isles. None of these men ever succeeded in finding a definitive solution to the problem. None of the ethnographers and ethnogenists, who joined in this search for the precise proportions of British, Celtic, Roman, Saxon, Danish, and Norman blood in Victorian veins, could be described as disinterested in their findings, let alone faultless in their methods. Whether they considered themselves amateurs or professionals, and the distinction between the two in the nineteenth century is not easily drawn, most of them relied on physiognomy as well as language and artifacts to buttress their particular version of the ethnogenesis of those who inhabited the British Isles.[32]

The results of these researches into the origins of what were known as "the races of Britain" ranged from scientific fiction to the supposedly hard data of anthropometric measurements. Only the exceptional investigator dared to rehabilitate the tarnished image of the Irish Celt in the course of this ethnological exercise; but Richard Tuthill Massy, M.D., Lecturer at the Royal College of Surgeons of Ireland, was an exceptional man. After considerable experience in the dissecting rooms of the British Isles and Paris, Massy wrote a book called *Analytical Ethnology* which was published in 1855.[33] Determined to rescue the Celts of Great Britain and Ireland from the lowly position assigned to them by Anglo-Saxons, Massy carried the so-called physiognomical method to an extreme, or rather to the extremities, by arguing with the aid of line drawings that the hands and feet of the Celts were far more delicate, shapely, and "eloquent" in movement than were those of Saxons. It followed, therefore, that Celts were superior to Saxons in more than this respect. Because Massy's style and method represent the quintessence of Victorian physiognomy, a few passages from his treatise deserve to be quoted:

There is one characteristic of the Celt and Saxon, not mentioned, that I have for years remarked; I mean the large calf and fore-arm, with the small thigh and arm of the former, and the small calf and fore-arm, with a large thigh and arm of the latter. Let me, however, be understood as speaking of these parts in proportion. With the large calf of the Celtic woman you have a small breast; with the large thigh of the Saxon woman you have a large breast. The

16

thigh and arm are shorter in the Saxon than in the Celt; the fore-arm and leg are longer in the Saxon than in the Celt. The leg and foot of the Celt are beautiful, the elastic, graceful walk, matchless. The leg and foot of the Saxon are abominable, as is seen in the heavy, awkward gait, of course admitting of many exceptions, which are the result of continual inter-marriages, so conducive to a healthy offspring of mental and corporeal vigour. . . .

The Celtic hand and foot are more graceful than the Saxon. The anterior curved line from the waist to the knee is most beautiful in the Celtic woman. The posterior curved line from the waist to the insertion of the hamstring muscles is most beautiful in the Saxon woman. The lateral curved line from the arm-pit to the ankle is most beautiful in the Celtic man. The Saxon woman's chest is lovely. The eye has no resting place. It is all so agreeably proportioned and so elegant as to be faultless. But the Celtic neck speaks its easy and graceful movements, particularly visible when supporting a well-proportioned head, and a pleasing, happy face.

 The Celtic woman's shoulders and that curved line from the ear to the insertion of the deltoid muscle, are filled with charms.[34]

Massy's work ranged well beyond female anatomy. He quoted his cousin's learned opinion, formed on the basis of serving with the army in Jamaica, that there were striking similarities between the inhabitants of Connaught and Africa. And he blamed such Anglo-Saxon papers as *The Times* for defaming Irish Celts and misleading English readers as to the true nature of that remarkably gifted people.[35] Massy was, of course, somewhat more passionate as well as clinical in his observations than most Victorian ethnologists, but wishful thinking and first impressions characterized many discussions about the morphology and mental traits of the Victorians' ancestors. For every flattering portrait of Irish Celtic physiognomy, usually drawn by someone who took pride in the "Celtic blood" running in his veins, there were ten treatises stressing the superior looks, faculties, and achievements of the Saxon, German, or Teutonic races.

One of the more revealing examples of the method used by Victorian ethnologists and anthropologists to prove their points may be found in a paper read by Daniel Mackintosh, Fellow of the Geological Society, before the Anthropological Society of London in 1865. For several years this genteel geologist, topographer, and student of mankind had toured the countryside of England and Wales taking notes on both the terrain and the physiognomies of the people he encountered. Mackintosh's samples of head shapes and faces may have been small, but his ambition was large, and he did not hesitate to make clear-cut distinctions between and among ethnic groups. The dichotomy between Gael and Saxon which emerged from Mackintosh's observations of ethnic types became one of the standard allusions for those Victorians who wished to contend that Irishmen were as different as possible from the other inhabitants of the British Isles. The Gaelic type discovered by Mackintosh in the remoter parts of Wales and Cornwall could easily be recognized by the following features:

17

Bulging forward of lower part of face—most extreme in upper jaw. Chin more or less retreating . . . (in Ireland the chin is often absent). Retreating forehead. Large mouth and thick lips. Great distance between nose and mouth. Nose short, upturned, frequently concave, with yawning nostrils.[36]

Like any good physiognomist, Mackintosh then went on to list the mental traits which accompanied these features. The Gaelic type, he declared, was:

Quick in perception, but deficient in depth of reasoning power; headstrong and excitable; tendency to oppose; strong in love and hate; at one time lively, soon after sad; vivid in imagination; extremely social, with a propensity for crowding together; forward and self-confident; deficient in application to deep study, but possessed of great concentration in monotonous or purely mechanical occupations, such as hop-picking, reaping, weaving etc.; want of prudence and foresight; antipathy to seafaring pursuits . . . veneration for authority.[37]

Contrast this arresting, if not arrested, figure with the archetypal Saxon as perceived by Mackintosh on his rambles through England:

Features excessively regular: face round, broad, and shortish, mouth well formed, and neither raised nor sunk. Chin neither prominent nor receding. Nose straight and neither long nor short. Underpart of face a short ellipse. Low cheek bones. Eyes rather prominent, blue or bluish grey and very well defined. Eyebrows semicircular, horizontally placed. Forehead semi-circular. . . . Flattened ears. Hair light brown. Chest and shoulders of moderate breadth. Tendency to obesity and rotundity. Short and round limbs, hands, and fingers. Total absence of all angles and sudden projections or depressions.

With this more harmonious and symmetrical face went the following temperamental traits:

Extreme moderation . . . absence of extraordinary talents and equal absence of extraordinary defects, mind equally balanced; character consistent, simple, truthful, straightforward and honest; persevering in pursuits admitting of variety, but unadapted to purely mechanical or monotonous occupations; predilections for agriculture; determined, but not self-willed; self-reliant yet humble; peaceable, orderly, unexcitable, unambitious, and free from extravagance; not brilliant in imagination, but sound in judgment; great general benevolence accompanying little particular attachment. . . .[38]

Such a physiognomical contrast deserves the conventional dichotomy of black and white. And yet there was a touch of gray in Mackintosh's depiction of the Saxon that can be accounted for only by assuming that he was, at heart, a staunch Scottish nationalist.

Mackintosh's venture into physiognomy did not provoke any serious rebuttal. Like most members of the Anthropological Society, he believed that substantial differences divided Saxons from Celts and Gaels and that those differences reached back to prehistoric times as a result of the laws of hereditary transmission of characteristics from one generation to the next within any given racial unit.[39] Lacking tangible evidence about the earliest inhabitants of the British Isles and confronted with a variety of ethnic types in the country, these comparative ethnologists regarded pigment and especially the color of hair and eyes as vital clues to the ethnic composition of the British people, past and present. They blended anthropology, ethnogeny, craniology, physiognomy, and ancient history, including the writings of Strabo, Tacitus, and Caesar, in order to arrive at a meaningful taxonomy of the races of Britain.

Physiognomical differentiation was the touchstone of most practicing anthropologists and ethnologists in the 1860s and 1870s. The Reverend Wentworth Webster reported to the Anthropological Institute in 1872 on the physical and mental traits of Basques, black Celts, and fair Celts in Spain. The black Celts in both Spain and Ireland, he asserted, were distinguished by a "lower facial angle, and a tendency to prognathism in the jaw." They shared in common with the Basque, moreover, a passion for gambling.[40] Another anthropologist, Hector Maclean of Islay in the Hebrides, delineated four basic types of Celt in Britain, ranging from the tall dolichocephalic to the short, dark "Sancho Panza" category. Like his compatriot Mackintosh, he relied on differences of pigment, shape of skull and face, posture, gait, as well as temperament for his criteria of ethnicity.[41] While these men combed the countryside for new data to fit their categories, other comparative ethnologists were making physiognomic distinctions between Kimmerians and Atlanteans, Finns and Lapps, Kabyles and Berbers as well as between the "ethnic effeteness" of French Celts and the muscular might of their Teutonic conquerors during the Franco-Prussian war.[42] If there was less divination in Victorian physiognomy compared with that of the classical school, the basic assumptions of that science and art still survived.

In some respects the most impressive of these Victorian ethnologists was Dr. John Beddoe (1826–1911) of Bristol, founding member of the Ethnological Society and later president of the Anthropological Institute from 1889 to 1891.[43] Beddoe devoted more than thirty years to the observation and measurement of physical features among the populations of Great Britain, Ireland, and Western Europe. He shared Francis Galton's commitment to quantitative analysis, although the two men differed markedly in their methods and statistical abilities. Beddoe's stature as an ethnologist rests primarily on his meticulous collection of morphological data in the field. A tireless investigator of ethnic and racial types in every part of the British Isles, Beddoe went well beyond the unsystematic physiognomical rambles of the Reverend Thomas Price and Daniel Mackintosh, and his labors were praised by several prominent American anthropologists in the 1950s.[44]

Beddoe believed that color of hair and eyes in man contained the key to ethnic or subracial origins. His so-called "Index of Nigrescence" was designed to quantify the amount of residual melanin in the skin or corium and

19

in the iris of the eye as well as the follicles of the hair. Beddoe explained the index as follows:

> A ready means of comparing the colours of two peoples or localities is found in the Index of Nigrescence. The gross index is gotten by subtracting the number of red and fair-haired persons from that of the dark-haired, together with twice the black-haired. I double the black, in order to give its proper value to the greater tendency to melanosity shown thereby; while brown (chestnut) hair is regarded as neutral, though in truth most of the persons placed in B are fair skinned, and approach more nearly in aspect to the xanthous than to the melanous variety.

$$D + 2N - R - F = \text{Index}$$

> From the gross index, the net, or percentage index, is of course readily obtained.[45]

Like Camper's facial angle, Beddoe's index was not only a speciously scientific device, but it implied that one end of the scale was preferable to the other. The index of nigrescence was a carefully contrived formula for measuring the ratio of black, brown, and red, as well as fair-haired persons in any given region. It served to confirm the impressions of many Victorians that the Celtic portions of the population in Wales, Cornwall, Scotland, and Ireland were considerably darker or more melanous than those descended from Saxon and Scandinavian forebears. There was much substance to this impression, and few men disputed Beddoe's findings. But he pushed his evidence and the index too vigorously. Beddoe had found that the index rose steadily as he moved from east to west in England and Ireland, and the highest index of all—well over 70 percent on his scale—was found in parts of Wales and western Ireland. Beddoe was no strident racist in the tradition of Gobineau, Knox, Hunt, Madison Grant, or H. S. Chamberlain. But he did inject a host of ethnocentric and elitist attitudes into his work on the racial makeup of the British Isles. His contrast between the fairer and orthognathous upper classes of both islands and the more melanous and prognathous workers of Wales and Ireland must have provided some reassurance to his fair-haired and dolichocephalic readers. The darkest, most prognathous Celts encountered on his trips inspired Beddoe to speculate on their African genesis, and he chose the term "Africanoid" to describe this extreme type with its jutting jaw and "long slitty nostrils." Doubtless there were cases of acute prognathism in Ireland, not to mention England and Scotland; but it required an ethnocentric imagination to find traces of an African genesis only in the Celtic core of South Wales and Munster.

Beddoe's index of nigrescence and his category of Africanoid Celts put the finishing touches on the later Victorian image of the Irish. The more familiar and amusing Paddy of stage, song, and cartoon had given way to a Celtic Caliban who seemed incapable of appreciating Anglo-Saxon civilization. When Englishmen added to their older image of the Irish such scientifically verified attributes as melanous and prognathous features, receding foreheads, and upturned noses, they were bound to come up with a composite caricature of a Caucasian Negro with simian features.

The net effect of Victorian ethnology, as professed and practiced in these years, was to undermine the environmentalist view that Englishmen and Irishmen were fundamentally alike and equally educable. Instead of narrowing the gap between Anglo-Saxons and Celts, the newer forms of evolutionary thought associated with Darwin, Wallace, Huxley, and their disciples, tended to polarize Englishmen and Irishmen by providing a scientific basis for assuming that such characteristics as violence, poverty, improvidence, political volatility, and drunkenness were inherently Irish and only Irish. The increasing reliance of European and British anthropologists on morphological measurement with the object of distinguishing as well as ranking the races of the world on the basis of cephalic, facial, and chromatic indexes had the predictable effect of relegating Negroes, Chinese, Indians, and other non-Caucasians to the lower limbs of the proverbial tree of human civilizations. Given the amount of prejudice in England and Scotland against the Irish in general and Irish immigrant workers in particular, it is hardly surprising that Celtic Irishmen should have found themselves occupying a branch which was closer in some respects to the Negro limb than to the Anglo-Saxon crown of that tree.

The widespread belief in Victorian England that Englishmen and Irishmen were separated by clear-cut ethnic or racial as well as religious and cultural barriers was reinforced continually by political events in both countries. Intermittent rebellions and chronic agrarian unrest in Ireland, combined with the disorderly behavior of some Irishmen in Britain, seemed to confirm the notion that Irish Celts were a subrace or people with habits antithetically opposed to English norms of thought and behavior. Nothing fed the Victorian stereotype of the wild, melancholic, violent, and feckless Irish Celt more dramatically than the economic stagnation and political and social unrest which English tourists and officials found in Ireland. Every abortive rebellion and every agrarian outrage helped to confirm the stereotype of Paddy as the ignorant and superstitious dupe of crafty leaders sworn to drive the "vile Sassenach" from the land by terrorist methods.

There was, moreover, relatively little dispassionate reporting of Irish affairs in English newspapers during these decades. Some measure of the hostility of *The Times* of London to Irish national aspirations may be gained from the fact that in the later 1880s almost one half of all Irish news items reported in that paper concerned what the government classified as "Special Crime"; namely, offenses arising out of agrarian and political motives.[46] Without any qualms about the inadequacy of their sample, many Victorians jumped to the conclusion that Irish Celts were born criminals at best and anarchists poorly trained in the use of dynamite and daggers at worst. The criminal dimension of Irish character was used to explain away the rising of '98 as well as Fenian outrages in the later 1860s and the land war in the next two decades. During the twenty years between the outbreak of Fenian activity and the height of the Parnellite agitation in the mid-1880s, the English image of politicized Paddy became even more bestial and simian. These were also the years when tens of thousands of post-famine Irish immigrants in Scotland and England were beginning to make their presence felt in a political sense, having already left their mark on British society and the economy. As militant Irish nationalists began to organize more effectively into constitutional parties and revolutionary brotherhoods sworn to secrecy, the stereotypes of Irish Celts in literature and caricature took on many of the features of apes with marked criminal tendencies. The price paid by Irishmen for increasing political activity and agrarian protest was the substitution of epithets like Caliban, Frankenstein, Yahoo, and gorilla for Paddy.

CHAPTER III

Victorian
Comic Art

TURNING FROM THE SCIENCE OF MAN to the art of caricature, we find that Irish Celts were among the favorite objects of satire and parody by Victorian comic artists. English caricature contained not only the elements of physiognomy already mentioned, but also many of the same features found in contemporary ethnological writings about the Irish. This is not the place to attempt a comprehensive study of Victorian caricature, however tempting and in need of explication that subject may be. Several recent works on the psychological and sociological aspects of caricature have included some of the more famous English comic artists, but on the whole the history of French, German, and American caricature during the nineteenth century has been better served by modern scholars than the English variety.[47] Recent publications on Victorian caricature and comic weeklies in the provincial capitals of Great Britain are scarce, and the comic art produced in Dublin during the Victorian era remains an almost wholly unexplored field. The glimpses of Irish stereotypes in English, American, and Irish comic periodicals in this book are no substitute for the intensive and wide-ranging study that is needed, but they may contain a few clues about the nature and function of one ethnic stereotype in Victorian cartoons and caricatures.

Distinctions between the terms caricature and cartoon may look impressive in dictionaries and learned journals, but in practice the dividing line between the two often becomes a matter of taste. Caricature, derived from the seventeenth-century Italian *caricatura*, is considerably older than the popular meaning of cartoon, denoting a comic drawing, which dates roughly from the 1840s. Some dictionaries stress the *grotesque* quality of caricature and the *comic* content of cartoons. But these two adjectives often merge or coexist in the same drawing, and people are bound to disagree about the effect of an artist's attempt to distort reality. Since the political cartoons of the Victorian era usually contain figures that are both grotesque and comic, cruel and ludicrous, pathetic and provoking, the terms will be used here as overlapping in meaning, if not exactly synonymous. In Victorian England, the terms were confused by some and rigidly separated by others. The position of principal or senior cartoonist on *Punch* was held for over forty years by Sir John Tenniel (1820–1914) who always insisted that he was a cartoonist on the grounds that his work was more humorous than grotesque. And yet Tenniel's representations of Irish political agitators and other

TIME'S WAXWORKS.

(1881 *JUST ADDED TO THE COLLECTION.*)

Mr. P. "HA! YOU'LL HAVE TO PUT HIM INTO THE CHAMBER OF HORRORS!"

4 "Time's Waxworks." In this New Year's Eve cartoon, Tenniel represents 1881 as the year of the Irish terrorist or dynamiter. Father Time introduces Mr. Punch to the latest and most ape-like figure in his waxworks collection, which is made up of annual imperial "problems." (*Punch*, 31 December 1881.)

"undesirables" were just as grotesque as those of Thomas Nast who is nowadays called a caricaturist. Another outstanding Victorian artist who also worked for *Punch*, Harry Furniss (1854–1925), once defined a caricaturist as "an artistic contortionist. He is grotesque for effect.... The good points of his subject must be plainly apparent to him before he can twist his study into the grotesque."[48] Caricature may have a more sophisticated sound to the ear than cartoon, but there is little to choose between the terms where the stereotypical Irish agitator was concerned.

Physiognomy is as inseparable from caricature as the stereotype is indispensable to any form of prejudice. One might even define political caricature as a pattern of graphic stereotypes informed by physiognomy and serving a satirical function. However timeless some aspects of caricature may be, there were certain values and beliefs which in their combinations were more

THE FENIAN-PEST.

Hibernia. "O MY DEAR SISTER, WHAT *ARE* WE TO DO WITH THESE TROUBLESOME PEOPLE?"
Britannia. "TRY ISOLATION FIRST, MY DEAR, AND THEN———"

5 *"The Fenian Pest."* Tenniel returns to the theme of the virago Britannia defending the chaste Hibernia from the clutches of Irish-American Fenians with huge jaws and low facial angles. (*Punch*, 3 March 1866.)

or less unique to the middle decades of the nineteenth century, and it is these special features which found their way into the faces of Irish Celts and several other categories of men as rendered by some of the comic artists and book illustrators of the time. Two of the most renowned illustrators of that or any other age, George Cruikshank (1792–1878) and Tenniel, whose careers spanned almost the entire century, relied constantly on the physiognomical equation of prognathism and savagery, if not bestiality, when they sought to epitomize Irish rebels and republicans. Much the same equation was used by many of Tenniel's fellow cartoonists in both London and New York, especially during and after the 1860s when the Fenian movement was being roundly condemned by all believers in the sanctity of Anglo-Saxon law and order. Like physiognomy, caricature operates out of the assumption once expressed by Lord Kames that "the character of a man may be read in his face." James Gillray (1757–1815), one of the founding fathers of modern political caricature, made the connection explicit in the 1790s, when he drew his "Doublures of Character, or Striking Resemblances of Physiognomy" and quoted Lavater's dictum: "If you would know men's hearts look in their faces." Among the facial pairs in this parody were the features of Charles James Fox which had so impressed Lavater himself.[49] The art of the caricaturist, then, lies in his ability to distort, and thereby draw attention to, those features of face and body which seem to him to epitomize the personality and character of the individual or group in question. Unlike the Lavaterian physiognomist, the caricaturist seeks to provoke —occasionally to shock—his viewers. The effect of his distortions may be short-lived, seen one day and forgotten the next. In some cases, however, a caricature may retain its ability to provoke long after the artist's immediate inspiration has passed. The greatest of the Victorian comic illustrators succeeded in tempering their moral indignation and political commitments with touches of the whimsical and the absurd.

One of the often overlooked by-products of Western urban culture in the middle decades of the nineteenth century was the emergence of the penny comic weekly, (which often cost two pence or more when stamped). This periodical should not be confused with its cousin the weekly illustrated journal which contained a mixture of topical articles, current reportage, some political gossip, and much fiction in the form of short stories, poems, and romantic novelettes serialized for weeks on end. Published in Fleet Street or the Strand, such journals as *The Illustrated London News, Cassell's Illustrated Family Paper, The Illustrated Times*, and *The Penny Illustrated Paper* all carried black-and-white lithographs and engravings which sought to enhance rather than to distort reality. Respectable readers who wanted a break from the solid and portentous columns of *The Times* turned to these pictorial potpourris which, with their splendidly colored Christmas supplements, were the direct forebears of the glossy magazines of the twentieth century. Some periodicals, it is true, tried to combine the illustrated reporting of *The Illustrated London News* with the feature cartoons of *Punch*, but hybrids like *Harper's Weekly* were the exception that proved the rule.

The new comic weeklies of the 1840s and after were blatantly frivolous and no less clean and decent than their more intellectual relations. Their purpose was to titillate and amuse; to sharpen the wits rather than to improve the mind. In general, their editors published more serious fiction only when they ran out of something irreverent and flippant to say, and that was not often. In an age without radio and television, these comic weeklies were the cheapest form of armchair entertainment for the essentially middle- and upper-middle-class reader. In content and format, they were far removed from the fortnightly and monthly literary reviews such as *The Edinburgh*, *The Quarterly*, and *The Contemporary* reviews with which highbrow Victorians nourished their minds. If the average life span of these Victorian comic weeklies was short, new ventures kept springing up in Fleet Street and the Strand to take the place of those that had succumbed to financial pressures. In London, such weeklies as *Punch* (launched in 1841), *Fun* (1861–1901), *Tomahawk* (1867–70), *Judy* (1867–1907), *Will-O-the-Wisp* (1868–69?), *Funny Folks* (1874–94), *Moonshine* (1879–1902), and *Ally Sloper's Half Holiday* (1884–88?) amused countless readers of all ages, but of these only *Punch* survived beyond the Edwardian era. And *Punch* owed its initial success more to the shrewd financial management of Messrs. Bradbury, Evans, and Agnew, the publishing firm, than to the special comic gifts of its staff.[50] In Dublin, the financial outlook for comic weeklies was even bleaker. A city so much smaller and poorer than London could hardly support comic periodicals for any length of time, and not one weekly lasted more than two years without folding or changing proprietor. In both England and Ireland, the comic weeklies contained as wide a range of topical nonsense, silly jokes, gossip, doggerel, and illustrations as the writers and artists could manage to invent, borrow, or steal. Diligent editors tried hard to attract readers with prize competitions, puzzles, political tidbits, lavish Christmas numbers, and even ladies' columns. Taking into account both the writing and the cartoons as well as the advertisements, these periodicals make a rich and relatively unexplored source for the study of the emerging metropolitan cultures of Western Europe, the British Isles, and America.

All of these comic weeklies employed artists, otherwise called lithographers, engravers, designers, illustrators, or cartoonists, whose job it was to lure readers with their comic sketches and serious cartoons. Most of these men were jacks and some were masters of several trades, having to supplement their meager earnings by illustrating books, moonlighting as lithographers and engravers, and even writing some of the doggerel and anecdotage that filled so many columns in the weeklies. Many cartoonists spent their lives jumping—or swimming—from one sinking periodical to another in the hope of finding a safe berth. The few who were invited to join the famous Table at *Punch* were fortunate indeed to have found a winner. Only two or three comic artists were able to make enough of a reputation while still young to strike off on their own as freelance cartoonists or as proprietors of their own weeklies. Not surprisingly, several of London's best cartoonists emigrated to America where publishers like Frank Leslie offered bigger salaries and better security.

Most of these Victorian comic weeklies carried a feature cartoon which occasionally covered two full pages and could be easily removed for posting or framing. Depending on the technical facilities and financial resources of the periodical, this cartoon could be printed in black and white or color— once chromolithography had become commercially feasible. The best known English weeklies stayed with black-and-white illustrations long after vivid colors had begun to suffuse their equivalents in America. The principal cartoon was usually the one serious or didactic note in the comic weekly, and given any degree of sympathy between editor and cartoonist on the great issues of the day, these graphic editorials would range in subject matter from prostitution and drink to war and peace. At *Punch* the entire staff gathered around the Table every Wednesday evening to eat and drink heartily and also to decide on the themes for both the senior and junior cartoons, which were always supposed to complement one another.[51] In the hands of a Tenniel or Matt Morgan, the political and social cartoon possessed more thrust than a first or second "leader" in *The Times* of London, and every cartoon worthy of the name conveyed its message to the viewer in a small fraction of the time it took to wade through a long-winded editorial. The principal cartoonist of a comic weekly was not a professional comedian, and he often wielded considerable influence, as Boss Tweed was quick to attest after Thomas Nast had turned his attention to the profound corruption at Tammany Hall. Feature cartoons, however, served more than the negative function of exposing the vices of men and the absurdities of party politics. They also helped to keep alive and promote certain values and ideals to which the editor and his staff subscribed. Take the example of the constitutional agitation for Irish Home Rule in the 1880s and 1890s, to which cause a number of Dublin's comic artists made contributions which have yet to be recognized by modern Irish historians.

The principal cartoonists of London, Dublin, and New York, to mention only those metropolitan areas involved in this study, sought to "mythologize the world by physiognomizing it," as E. H. Gombrich has written.[52] At times they also cut through or exposed mythologies by emphasizing the capacity of men to deceive themselves as well as others. Like most men, needless to say, cartoonists were quite capable of substituting new myths for old. In the case of Tenniel and at least a dozen other prominent cartoonists in London and New York, the Irish Celt—especially in his militantly political phase— became a favorite object of that mythologizing process with physiognomical results that could hardly be described as allaying the widespread prejudices that already weighed heavily on Irish Catholics in the nineteenth century.

28

CHAPTER IV

Simianizing the Irish Celt

DURING THE FIRST TWO-THIRDS of the nineteenth century the stereotypical Paddy or Teague of English cartoon and caricature underwent a significant change. In sharp contrast to the regular, even handsome features of the "wild Irishman" or woodkern of the Elizabethan and early Stuart period, such as may be found in abundance in John Derricke's *The Image of Irelande, with a Discouerie of Woodkarne*, first published in 1581,[53] and different, too, from the brutish, slovenly faces of Irish peasants appearing in prints dating from the reign of George III, the dominant Victorian stereotype of Paddy looked far more like an ape than a man. In less than a century, Paddy had become a monstrous Celtic Caliban capable of any crime known to man or beast. By the 1860s no respectable reader of comic weeklies—and most of their readers were respectable—could possibly mistake the simous nose, long upper lip, huge, projecting mouth, and jutting lower jaw as well as sloping forehead for any other category of undesirable or dangerous human being than that known as Irish. Out of the confusion of ethnic, political, and national stereotypes in eighteenth-century caricature, the Irish Celt finally emerged in the mid-Victorian period with his own inimitable and unenviable identity.

The process of simianizing Paddy's features took place roughly between 1840 and 1890 with the 1860s serving as a pivotal point in this alteration of the stereotype. In both England and America the simianized version of the Irish Celt lasted well into the twentieth century, only to die out slowly after the rebellion and intermittent warfare of 1916–21. The beginnings of this new stereotype are less easily defined. The simian or ape-like Celt of the Victorian era did not spring full-blown from the head of any particular cartoonist working in the 1860s. The antecedents of this stereotype were just as widespread as the conviction in England and Scotland that the Irish were inherently inferior and quite unfit to manage their own affairs. The changes in Paddy's features during the middle decades of the century do seem to reflect a change in attitude among many Victorians about Irishmen and Irish agitation. More revealing in some respects than the overall change in Paddy's physiognomy was the rate of that change, although no precise time can be assigned to a process of gradual and occasionally inconsistent alteration of facial traits. Identifying the period of greatest change in the stereotype may, however, tell us something about the underlying causes, just as the nature of the change may reveal some of the preoccupations of the artists responsible for those changes.

Any inquiry into Irish stereotypes in Victorian caricature ought to begin with those outstanding social and political caricaturists of the later eighteenth century, Thomas Rowlandson (1756–1827) and James Gillray (1757–1815). When these men were not busy caricaturing Georgian society as well as George III and his politicians, they occasionally drew faces which appear to be the distant ancestors of the Fenian ape-men of the 1860s and after. Scattered through Gillray's splendid satires of English, not to mention French, political life are the figures of rioters, radicals, and rebels with long faces, wild eyes, snub noses, flaring nostrils, cavernous mouths, and jutting jaws. Gillray drew several such faces in his caricatures of French Jacobins in the early 1790s and again in his famous series of drawings depicting the fate of Englishmen in the event of a successful French invasion. Among the soldiers in his "Promised Horrors of the French Invasion" (20 October 1796) and in the four plates on the theme, "The Consequences of a Successful French Invasion" (1 March 1798), may be seen both protoprognathous and acutely prognathous features which any student of Lavater would associate with brutal and vicious behavior.[54] And Gillray, as we have suggested, knew his Lavater. It is important to note, however, that the prognathous faces drawn by both Rowlandson and Gillray had no specific ethnic or national identity. Such features were meant to convey the swinishness of the multitude, especially the primitive instincts of the politicized "mob," whether English, Scottish, Irish, or European. The beginnings of a more positive connection between this facial type and Irishmen date from the insurrection of 1798, when Gillray filled several of his topical drawings with brutish Irish peasants wielding pikes and bearing the facial traits of an aroused rabble: large, grizzled jaws, bulging eyes, and wide margin between snub nose and thick upper lip.[55]

The bloody rising of 1798 in Ireland did not in itself forge any binding link between Irishmen and prognathous features in English imaginations. Brutish expressions were conferred by various cartoonists on rioters and radicals at home and abroad, and there was nothing specifically Irish about a projecting lower jaw until the 1840s, when thousands of Irish immigrants were pouring into England and Scotland, most of them destitute and many of them diseased. Both Isaac Cruikshank (1756?–1811?), the Scottish born illustrator, and his talented sons, Robert (1789–1856) and George (1792–1878), all of whom knew Gillray and his work, assigned these facial features to non-Irish types in the early 1800s; and in 1819, George, the most famous member of this artistic family, drew several such faces in his etching, "Death or Liberty! or Britannia & the Virtues of the Constitution in Danger" (1 December 1819).[56] During the first third of the nineteenth century, then, the elongated and prognathous face lacked any specific national identity, even though it became increasingly associated with the agitation of Irishmen against tithes, for Catholic emancipation, and, later, for repeal of the Act of Union of 1800. The popular notion of the "swinish" mob or multitude

30

may help to account for the faintly—at times markedly—porcine features, especially around the cheeks, nose, and mouth, which cartoonists of the time often assigned to radical or revolutionary agitators. Because pigs played such a vital part in the Irish peasant economy, it was all too easy for comic artists to equate Irish rebels with the lean, even emaciated pigs of the countryside and to endow United Irishmen with snouts instead of noses.

During the 1840s the acutely prognathous face became more and more identified with Irish peasants, whether or not they happened to be ardent rebels. After the launching of *Punch, Or the London Charivari* in 1841, the equation between snub-nosed, big-mouthed, and prognathous faces and Irish Celts became as complete as caricature could hope to achieve. Although *Punch's* artists did not really warm to their task of drawing Irish peasants with hyperprognathous features until the later 1840s and 1850s, it soon became clear that Irishmen, in particular the more politicized among them, were the favorite target of both writers and cartoonists. Marion H. Spielmann, the chronicler of *Punch*, wrote that the comic weekly acquired a reputation for being anti-Irish during and after the 1850s. But he was quick to point out that *Punch* always showed sympathy for "what he considered genuine Irish sentiment and suffering." When Irishmen turned to political agitation and began to demand an end to British rule, then *Punch* changed his tune, and, according to Spielmann, the artists began to "picture the Irish political outrage-mongering peasant as a cross between a garrotter and a gorilla."[57] What Spielmann failed to point out was that the stereotypical Irishman of *Punch* looked like a prognathous garroter in the 1840s and like a gorilla in the 1860s. Indeed, the only Celt to be flattered and admired by *Punch's* cartoonists was "Hibernia," the intensely feminine symbol of Ireland, whose haunting beauty conveyed some of the sufferings of the Irish people.

One of *Punch's* leading cartoonists in the early years was Joseph Kenny Meadows (1790–1874), who drew the first feature cartoon of an "Irish Frankenstein" in the issue of 4 November 1843.[58] Meadows's attempt to ridicule the repeal movement represents one more step in the direction of simianizing Paddy, but for all his grotesque features, which included flaring nostrils, protruding lower lip, receding chin, and small horns, this prancing "Frankenstein" was neither a gorilla nor an orangutan. The effect of this creature on the viewer is markedly different from that of the simianized Celts who appeared in the 1860s and after.

John Leech (1817–64), whose father was of "Irish extraction," drew many of the principal cartoons in the 1840s and 1850s which saved *Punch* from artistic mediocrity. Leech was a gifted cartoonist and a keen student of Irish physiognomy, but not all of his Paddies were prognathous brutes, as may be seen from his cartoon, "The 'Repeal Farce'."[59] On more than one occasion, however, he resorted to a simian metaphor in an Irish context. The militancy of the Young Ireland movement after the death of Thomas Davis inspired

31

THE IRISH FRANKENSTEIN.

6 *The Irish Frankenstein.*" In 1843 the *Punch* cartoonist J. Kenny Meadows depicted Daniel O'Connell as Dr. Frankenstein conjuring up a monstrous Irish peasant complete with horns, flaring nostrils, and thick lips, who was supposed to epitomize the new movement for repeal ("Repale") of the Act of Union. (*Punch*, 4 November 1843.)

32

THE "REPEAL FARCE;"

OR, MOTHER GOOSE AND THE GOLDEN EGGS.

7 *The 'Repeal Farce'.*" Paddy in his pre-simian phase. In this drawing which appeared in *Punch* in 1843, John Leech endowed Paddy with an upturned nose and prognathous jaw, but the total effect is that of a grotesque Celtic man rather than an ape. (*Punch*, volume 4, page 37.)

Leech to turn John Mitchel, one of the outspoken extremists (whose name *Punch* misspelled for several months) into a complete monkey. In "The British Lion and the Irish Monkey" (8 April 1848), Mitchel was portrayed as an angry little monkey, no attempt being made by the artist to simianize his features. Wearing a jester's cap and carrying two pistols in his belt, this sharp-toothed creature was shown confronting the imperial lion which towered over him. The monkey was made to exclaim: "One of us MUST be Put Down."[60] Leech continued to characterize Mitchel as a vicious monkey constantly getting into scrapes, until Mitchel's arrest on a charge of treason-felony and his transportation overseas.[61] In 1848 Leech drew several cartoons crammed with Irish brutes, whose huge jaws, long upper lips, and simous noses expressed all too clearly the artist's opinion of Irishmen who dared to protest against famine conditions and British rule.[62] In technique, these hyperprognathous faces represented only a slight advance on the rebels of '98 drawn by Cruikshank a few years previously. But for all their prognathism, the rebels of '48 drawn by Leech looked more human than bestial. London's comic artists and illustrators had not yet discovered the Irish ape.

A good example of extreme prognathism in cartoons or drawings of Irish faces outside *Punch*, also dating from the 1840s, is an obscure little volume written and illustrated by Watts Phillips called *The Queen in Ireland*, published in London around 1849. The hero of this simple tale is a stereotypical Englishman named Smithers, a plump and myopic gentleman who runs into a number of snub-nosed and huge-jawed Paddies in the course of his wanderings through County Cork in a vain attempt to catch up with the Queen's entourage. After various misfortunes along the stage-Irish wayside, Smithers arrives at a small inn where he is stunned by a bottle thrown by one of the contestants in a proverbial Irish shindy. Smithers no sooner recovers from that blow than he is laid low by poteen which has a stupefying effect, and while unconscious he is robbed of all his money and clothes by a group of prognathous Paddies. After coming to his senses, the half-naked Smithers sets out on the road to Cork, firmly resolved never to leave the land of the Saxon again.[63]

More important in some respects than *Punch's* early caricatures of Irish faces were George Cruikshank's striking illustrations for W. H. Maxwell's *History of the Rebellion in Ireland in 1798*.[64] By the 1840s Cruikshank had reached a plateau of eminence as a book illustrator, and his services were much in demand. He had already illustrated dozens of best sellers, including all of the Waverley novels (the 1836–38 edition), and his work was admired by thousands of readers. For Maxwell's account of the atrocities committed by the ferocious rebels on "innocent" Protestants, Cruikshank drew some of the finest plates of his career. Highly reminiscent of Gillray's prints dealing with the rebellion of 1798 are Cruikshank's faces of the rebels in Counties Kildare and Wexford, some of which are reproduced here. These rebels allegedly impaled babies and drummer boys on their pikes and murdered

8 *The Image of '98*. George Cruikshank endowed the rebels of 1798 with distinctly brutish and prognathous features, when he drew the illustrations for W. H. Maxwell's history of the rebellion in 1798 (London, 1845). (Detail from "Murder of George Crawford and his Granddaughter" in *History of the Rebellion in Ireland in 1798*, page 66. Reprint, London, 1894.)

George Crawford and his granddaughter in cold blood. Given their puffy cheeks and exposed nostrils, some of these rebel faces strongly suggest the presence of a porcine ancestor. But the concave nose and wide gap between the nostrils and the mouth with its grotesque projection, also have something in common with the "Sancho Panza" Celts discovered by ethnologists in Wales and Ireland.[65] However brutish the faces of Irishmen found in British cartoons and illustrations during the 1840s and 1850s, Paddy remained essentially human in outward form until the 1860s, when the era of acute midfacial prognathism began to turn into the age of the simianized Celt.

The man who did most to change the Irish stereotype in English cartoons from man to beast was John Tenniel, who was born in 1820, knighted in 1893, and died in 1914.[66] Over a fifty-year period Tenniel drew some two

9 *The Image of '98*. The rebel pikemen of 1798 have distinctly prognathous features in this detail from George Cruikshank's illustration "The Loyal Little Drummer." (From W. H. Maxwell's *History of the Rebellion in Ireland in 1798*, page 115. Reprint, London, 1894.)

thousand cartoons for *Punch*, and these drawings constitute one of the splendors of Victorian popular culture. Born in Kensington, the son of a Huguenot fencing master or *maitre d'armes*, Tenniel studied art for several years with Charles Keene, who became a close friend. Like George Cruikshank and other cartoonists of his acquaintance, Tenniel earned both money and a reputation from book illustrating, and his drawings for an edition of *Aesop's Fables* in 1848 caught the eye of Mark Lemon, the influential editor of *Punch*, who soon invited him to join the staff. Tenniel did not begin to draw the feature cartoon on a regular basis until 1862, some ten years after joining *Punch*, and on the death of John Leech in 1864 he became principal cartoonist. His illustrations for the adventures of Alice may have displeased the irascible Lewis Carroll but they gained him lasting fame, and his work for *Punch* made him England's premier cartoonist until his retirement in

January 1901. The dignity of tone, authority, seriousness of purpose, and wry sense of humor which were his trademarks turned the senior cartoon or "big cut" into a weekly event that was anticipated far beyond the confines of Fleet Street. Credit for those cartoons should also go to *Punch's* writers who suggested so many of the topics which Tenniel brought to fruition and, indeed, to the engravers Swain and Dalziel who faithfully copied his drawings from wood blocks onto plates.

Tenniel played a major role in the change which Paddy's features underwent in cartoons after 1860. From Gillray to George Cruikshank the convention among cartoonists in London had been to increase Paddy's prognathism or rather to lower his facial angle, but the face had remained essentially human. In the 1860s, however, Paddy began to look like the offspring of a liaison between a gorilla father and a prognathous Irish mother; in short, more like a monster than a man. To understand this simianizing process requires a closer look at some of the cartoons and caricatures of Irish subjects in English comic weeklies after 1860.

For many comic artists of Tenniel's generation the advent of the revolutionary republican movement known as Fenianism, whose members were sworn to end British rule in Ireland by physical force, seemed to reveal the beast that lurked within Irish character. Fenian raids on police stations and small towns in Ireland in the later 1860s, most of which ended in imprisonment for the attackers and hundreds of their friends, inspired many cartoons in comic weeklies. Tenniel and his colleagues leaned heavily on the traditional theme of Beauty (Hibernia or Erin) being rescued from the clutches of the Beast (Fenianism) by a handsome Prince or St. George (Law and Order). In their efforts to play up the menace of Fenianism to English civilization, many cartoonists in London depicted Fenian Paddy as an apelike monster. In Tenniel's hands those who dared to defy British authority in Ireland were made to look like denizens of the jungle: Paddy thus passed from prognathism into simianism. After the sensational explosions and deaths at Clerkenwell and Manchester, when Fenians tried to liberate some of their captured leaders, Tenniel drew some grotesquely simianized Paddies for *Punch* including "The Order of the Day," "The Mad Doctor," and "The Fenian Guy Fawkes."[67] Other examples might be cited, but even at a glance these Irish stereotypes look less human and humane than the rebels of '98 drawn by Gillray and Cruikshank. Admittedly, Tenniel was kinder with his pencil to those Irishmen who recognized the benefits of British rule, and his ape-like Fenians should be compared with the honest, sturdy, firm-jawed but still slightly prognathous features of those Irishmen who are being sworn in as special constables by John Bull to cope with the Fenian rising in "A Hint to the Loyal Irish."[68]

During the 1870s Tenniel drew fewer ape-like Irishmen as *Punch* concentrated his efforts on politics at Westminster and European diplomacy, while hundreds of Fenians remained in jail. Toward the end of the decade,

10 *"The Mad Doctor."* In this contrived scene by John Tenniel, John Bull consoles Hibernia for having to endure the Fenian menace. Presumably he expects some reward from this Irish maiden for having subdued and incarcerated the "mad" Irishman with his vacant stare and long upper lip. (*Punch,* 8 June 1867.)

however, *Punch* began to take notice of agrarian crime in Ireland and of the more militant brand of nationalism espoused by Parnell and his friends. The combination of land war in Ireland and obstruction by Irish nationalist politicians in Parliament spurred English comic artists to turn Paddy even more thoroughly into an ape-like Caliban. In countless feature cartoons of the 1880s, the Land League was made to look as though its members were monstrous brutes without a touch of humanity. The high point of this second spate of simianizing occurred just after the assassination of Lord Frederick Cavendish and his Under Secretary in Phoenix Park on 6 May 1882. For several months after this notorious crime, London's comic weeklies were filled with cartoons of ape-like monsters with huge mouths and sharp fangs. Tenniel rose nobly to the occasion of agrarian crime and political murder in Ireland. In his "Two Forces" Britannia looks resolutely into the ugly face of a Fenian ape-man who is about to hurl a brick, and in his classic version of "The Irish Frankenstein" Tenniel spelled out the physiognomical equation between bestial features and the assumed savagery of Irish character.[69] In "The Irish Devil-Fish" Tenniel endowed the octopus,

11 *"The Fenian Guy Fawkes."* Tenniel increases the degree of prognathism in
this stereotype of a Fenian dynamiter, while playing on old anti-Catholic prejudices in his new version of the gunpowder plot. (*Punch*, 28 December 1867.)

FENIANISM
SPECIAL
CONSTABLES

A HINT TO THE LOYAL IRISH.

"AH, THIN, MISTHER BULL! GIVE US THE OATH AN' SOME O' THIM STICKS. SURE, THERE'S
HUNDHREDS O' THE BOYS AS IS READY TO HELP YE, SOR."

12 "*A Hint to the Loyal Irish.*" In this Tenniel cartoon, Constable John Bull
hands out batons to a group of sturdy and loyal Irishmen who have just been
sworn in as special constables in order to help with the suppression of Fenianism.
The faces of these Irishmen reveal the equation in Tenniel's mind between loyalty
to the Queen and high facial angles. (*Punch*, 4 January 1868.)

TWO FORCES.

13 *"Two Forces."* In this classic confrontation between the forces of good and evil, Tenniel shows Britannia protecting a distraught Hibernia from a stone-throwing Irish anarchist with repellent features. Trodding on the Land League and holding the sword of justice, Britannia serves notice that she will prosecute Irish criminal conspirators to the full extent of the law. (*Punch*, 29 October 1881.)

14 *Detail from "Two Forces."* This detail reveals the almost complete simianization of Paddy. Tenniel has given his villain such proverbially ape-like features as
the simous nose, long, projecting upper lip, shallow lower jaw, and fang-like teeth.
(*Punch*, 29 October 1881.)

THE IRISH FRANKENSTEIN.

"The baneful and blood-stained Monster * * * yet was it not my Master to the very extent that it was my Creature ? * * * Had I not breathed into it my own spirit ? " * * * (*Extract from the Works of* C. S. P-RN-LL, M.P.)

15 *"The Irish Frankenstein."* Tenniel's version of the Frankenstein theme appeared shortly after the Phoenix Park murders in 1882. The simianized assassin with pistol and dripping dagger in each hand stands next to a death notice signed by Captain Moonlight, the legendary leader and organizer of Irish agrarian crime. Tenniel's monster is meant to convey the essence of the "new departure" in Ireland. (*Punch*, 20 May 1882.)

43

THE IRISH DEVIL-FISH.

"The creature is formidable, but there is a way of resisting it. * * * The Devil-fish, in fact, is only vulnerable through the head."
VICTOR HUGO's *Toilers of the Sea*, Book IV., Ch. iii.

16 *"The Irish Devil-Fish."* Tenniel depicts Gladstone, when Prime Minister, struggling with the octopus-like Irish Land League, whose tentacles threaten to envelop him. The huge mouth and prognathous features leave no doubt as to the ethnicity or breeding ground of this octopus. (*Punch*, 18 June 1881.)

symbolizing Irish revolution, with which Gladstone is struggling, with distinctly simian features.[70] One of the great masters of animal cartoons, Tenniel often gave Irish rebels and dynamiters the bodies of dragons, snakes, and wild beasts, but he invariably assigned ape-like features to the face. One of Tenniel's most striking variations on the simian theme may be found in a little-known drawing he did around 1878 for an illustrated edition of Shakespeare which never materialized. Dominating this scene from "The Tempest" is the hideous figure of Caliban on his knees with ferocious mouth full of sharp teeth and with the nose and forehead of an ape.[71] This creature could only be first cousin to Tenniel's grotesque "O'Caliban" of 22 December 1883.[72]

In his cartoons of Irishmen caught up in the revolutionary movements of the 1860s and after, Tenniel turned the clock back to that point in biological time when the great apes evolved into man. If the Irish rebels of Gillray's imagination represented a case of arrested development, the Irish Frankensteins and Calibans of Tenniel and his colleagues spelled complete degeneration.

The simianized version of Paddy appeared in most of the other comic weeklies published in London during this period. In *Judy, Or the London Serio-Comic Journal*, which closely resembled *Punch* in both format and content, the editor, Charles Ross, and his principal cartoonist from 1867 to 1880, John Proctor, waged an impressive campaign against Fenianism. Proctor was one of the ablest political cartoonists of his day.[73] Born in Edinburgh in 1836, he worked for six years as apprentice to an engraver before moving to London in 1859. After illustrating books for the publishing firm of Cassell, he turned from woodcuts to cartoons and then moved from the short-lived *Will-o-the Wisp* to *Judy* in 1867. In 1881 he left *Judy* to become principal cartoonist of *Moonshine*, and after nine fruitful years with that weekly, he changed offices again, working first for *Funny Folks* and then for *Fun*. Proctor was a prodigious worker who often drew two or three feature cartoons every week, and he richly deserves the accolade of one admirer as being "a consummate draughtsman, a master of line."[74] Proctor had little time for Irish agitators, and he chose a favorite theme of British caricature when he drew "St. George and the Dragon" in which a handsome warrior in Roman armor riding a white charger is about to drive a spear marked "Law" into a gorilla-faced dragon, complete with Irish hat and clay pipe, labeled "Fenianism." The doggerel accompanying this cartoon made it clear what *Judy* thought of Fenianism:

> Tis a treacherous baste, with never a taste
> of honour, love, or pity,
> From Fenian name of old it came,
> But was hatched in New York City.[75]

Similarly, in his cartoon "'67, Move On!'" Proctor drew the figure of a prognathous and semi-simian Fenian armed with a rifle scurrying away from an English constable carrying a truncheon.[76] In "The Bogus American" much the same simian features appear again on a handcuffed Irish-American who has been detained in Her Majesty's custody.[77] Proctor's stirring cartoon, "St. Patrick Redivivus," sprawls over two pages and shows the patron saint expelling a horde of ape-like Fenians from his holy island.[78] Like Tenniel, Proctor was quite capable of drawing Irishmen with decent features when he wanted to show that there were still a few loyalists left in Ireland, but orthognathous Irish Celts are rarities amidst his heavily simianized Fenians and Land Leaguers.

By January 1881, *Judy* had acquired a new principal cartoonist named W. Bowcher, about whom little is known. Although his work tended to be less exacting than Proctor's, Bowcher had a flair for the dramatic situation, and he excelled at simianizing Paddy. During the early 1880s, when the Irish Land League and the terrorist society known as the Invincibles were making headlines and inspiring angry editorials in English newspapers, *Judy* characterized Gladstone as an incompetent prime minister and depicted the Land Leaguers as murderous gorillas. Some idea of *Judy's* obsession with the Irish question may be gained from the following head count: out of a total of fifty-three feature cartoons drawn by Bowcher in 1881, twenty-one contained the simianized faces of Irishmen, and the Irish question received far more attention than any other issue in these cartoons.[79] For the first six months of 1882 Bowcher drew both prognathous and simian Irishmen in nine out of twenty-six cartoons, and even his serpents and pigs, which were meant to symbolize Irish political crime, had simianized features.[80] In his double-page cartoon "Following An Established Precedent," Bowcher depicted two semi-simian brutes squaring off for a fight to the death in the manner of the Kilkenny cats, and it is significant that the anti-Land Leaguer on the left of this drawing has a straighter nose than his Parnellite opponent, although there is not much to choose between them in terms of the mouth and jaw.[81] Several months later, and almost two weeks after the imprisonment of the Land League's leaders, Bowcher produced a restatement of the St. George and the Dragon motif, but this time a few new wrinkles were added to Proctor's previous dragon, vintage 1867. Bowcher's hero on this occasion was a knight clad in armor who had just driven his lance through the midriff of a coiled dragon which had a masked face, reminiscent of the masks worn by many "Moonlighters" and other nocturnal raiding parties in Ireland. With its long upper lip and snarling mouth, this dragon represented the Land League which was about to turn on the beauti-ful figure of Hibernia, shown chained to a wall and clutching the infant Land Act of 1881 in her arms. St. George thus saved the dark-haired beauty from a fate worse than death; and the title of this cartoon, "At Last," signi-fied that a new coercion act and imprisonment were going to teach the Land League a lesson it would not soon forget.[82] During the Home Rule crisis of

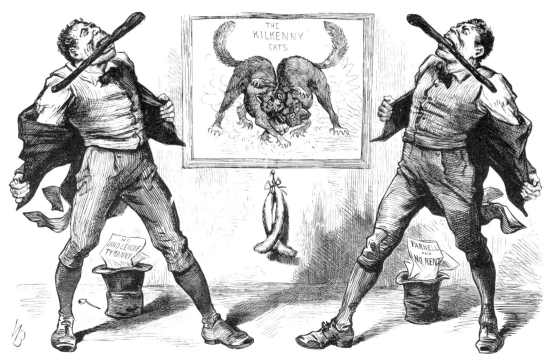

17 *"Following an Established Precedent."* W. Bowcher, cartoonist for *Judy*, depicts two Irishmen, one loyal and the other disloyal, but both equally wild and prognathous, about to fight in the best tradition of the Kilkenny cats—whose tails were the only remains of that historic encounter. (*Judy*, 8 June 1881.)

1886 Bowcher again filled his cartoons with ape-like Irishmen whose gaping mouths and sharp fangs were meant to suggest that the Irish were not quite ready to govern themselves.

In marked contrast to Bowcher's somber handling of the Irish menace, one of *Judy's* minor cartoonists, Archibald Chasemore, made great sport out of the simian idiom. Among the many small sketches he drew for *Judy* in the 1880s, there are two acutely ape-like Irish faces which belong to Paddies actively involved in the Land League. The features of "The Penniless Patriot," hoping for a handout in the name of the Land League, vaguely resemble a gorilla, while those of the creature shown greeting Parnell on his admission to Kilmainham jail have more in common with a chimpanzee. Their only resemblance to men lies in the hats, hair, tattered clothes, and pipes.[83] Two finer examples of the ape-like Paddy in cartoons would be hard to find.

English readers of comic weeklies could also find assorted shapes and sizes of simianized Celts from Ireland in such periodicals as *Ally Sloper's Half Holiday*, wherein W. G. Baxter, principal cartoonist from 1884 to 1886, produced some fine specimens of the Irish ape.[84] J. Stafford, who drew the

47

feature cartoon for *Funny Folks* in the 1880s, created a completely simian epitome of the Land League, holding a shillelagh and thumbing his snub-nose at a fierce bulldog labeled John Bull in his "Now, God Help Thee, Poor Monkey."[85] In "The Dragon and St. George" Stafford depicted the Land League as a scaly monster with the head of a wild boar astride a horse in the act of clubbing a figure representing British authority with the stock of his Fenian blunderbuss.[86] John Proctor, as we have seen, carried the simian-ized Irishman with him on his journey to *Moonshine* during the 1880s. And many lesser known cartoonists on the staffs of these humorous weeklies used the same device in their black-and-white sketches and "junior" cartoons. On the other hand, Paul Gray (1842–66), the brilliant cartoonist of *Fun* who died at the age of 24, deviated from the simian norm when he drew Irishmen with the faces of ruffians rather than apes in 1865–66. But then Gray was an Irishman. Other artists on the staff, however, indulged in the simianized idiom, and the ape-like Fenian or Land Leaguer began to appear regularly in *Fun* during the era of the Land League and the Phoenix Park murders.[87]

Toward the end of the 1860s some unforgettable versions of the Irish ape began to appear in the *Tomahawk*, an ostensibly comic weekly that packed into its three years of existence some of the finest cartoons and informed comment on politics and society of any Victorian weekly. The owner and chief cartoonist of this periodical—one of the first to experiment with color in the feature cartoon—was Matthew Somerville Morgan (1839–90), the son of an actor and actress-singer. Matt Morgan was both versatile and rest-less, studying at art schools in London, Paris, Italy, and Spain. Fond of travel, he made an excursion to Africa before settling down as a designer of scenery and cartoonist in London. After brief stints with the *Illustrated London News* and *Fun*, he launched the *Tomahawk, A Saturday Journal of Satire*, in 1867, but the circulation was too small to sustain the venture, possibly because the Queen came in for some pointed satire in several num-bers. Frank Leslie, the noted American entrepreneur and publisher, then persuaded Morgan to come to New York in 1870 to draw for his own *Illustrated Newspaper*, hoping thereby to create a rival for Thomas Nast. Morgan's fortunes improved noticeably after his arrival in America, and he embarked on several business ventures there, while producing both litho-graphs and watercolors. Shortly before his death, Morgan was appointed art editor of *Colliers, Once A Week*.[88]

One would have to look long and hard to find a face more sinister and a facial angle lower than Morgan's monster in "The Irish Frankenstein" which ranks with the best of the ape-men of horror films.[89] This was no ordinary simianized Paddy. Morgan created a human orangutan with the expression of a village idiot. This was the kind of monster one did not easily forget, and, as we will see, at least one comic artist in Dublin recalled it almost twenty-four years later.

In January 1870 Morgan ushered the new year in with his cartoon

18 *"The Irish Frankenstein."* Matt Morgan's Fenian monster, one of the finest examples of the Irish ape-man genre, awaits the Doctor's orders to strike terror into loyalist hearts. (*The Tomahawk,* 18 December 1869.)

19 "*Dissolving Views! Or, the Past and the Future.*" In Morgan's cartoon contrasting the political situation in Ireland and France from 1869 to 1870, Father Time projects two sets of lantern slides. The one on the left superimposes a prognathous and lethal Fenian on top of a carefree stage Irishman; and, on the right, a bellicose, flag-waving Napoleon III almost blots out a figure representing the once peace-loving Second Empire. (*The Tomahawk*, 15 January 1870.)

"Dissolving Views! Or, the Past and the Future," which neatly conveyed the process of making images, as the Irish stereotype changes from a frolicking Paddy to a simianized Celt from one lantern slide to the next.[90] In other cartoons on the subject of Fenianism, Morgan resorted to the dragon and reptile in order to epitomize the handiwork of Fenians, and most of these serpents had ape-like features.[91] Morgan's penchant for drawing Fenian monsters did not mean that he abhorred all Irishmen. The *Tomahawk* was no Tory tract or Whiggish weekly, and several front-page articles appealed for restraint and understanding in coping with the Irish difficulty. For many reasons, including the Morgan variations on the simianized Irish Celt, it is a shame that the *Tomahawk* did not last beyond 1870.

In order to show how closely some Victorian cartoonists adhered to the canons of craniology and physiognomy, as these were understood at the time, an attempt has been made to apply Pieter Camper's facial angle or index to some of the faces drawn by the artists represented here. Even a rough measurement of the facial angles of Fenians, Land Leaguers, harmless Paddies, English statesmen, and other categories makes it possible to record the degree of prognathism or orthognathism which cartoonists saw fit to

20 "*St. Dragon and the George.*" Morgan reverses the traditional roles of this famous legend and converts the Fenian dragon into a prognathous monster whose scales do not quite conceal his semi-simian ancestry. (*The Tomahawk*, 12 October 1867.)

bestow on their stereotypes. Using Camper's own criteria and prototypical measurements, one may gain some sense of the place of Paddy and his rulers in the hierarchy of man. The application of Camper's angle to the characters in these cartoons does, indeed, raise a number of technical problems, not all of which can be surmounted. It is impossible to obtain a reasonably accurate measurement unless the face is drawn in full profile and the ears and forehead are clearly exposed. Since so many of the Celtic Calibans and simian Fenians were drawn with matted hair hiding their ears and with hats or masks obscuring their upper faces, one must estimate at times where the key points used by Camper are located. Gladstone and Disraeli, moreover, were often drawn in clear profile, but cartoonists gave them such long locks of hair that the ears are completely hidden. The facial angle, moreover, does not reveal anything about the face as such except the relationship of the lower jaw to the frontal bone of the cranium. It was the device of an anatomist interested in bone structure, not of a physiognomist concerned with character as revealed by the contours and planes of the face. In spite of these imperfections, the application of Camper's measurement to some of the faces in Victorian cartoons does provide an indication of the gap that divided the Irish stereotype of the 1860s and after from the English ideal type designed in London.

Using the criteria laid down by Camper which were mentioned above, we have obtained an angle of approximately 68° for the figure of "Anarchy" in Tenniel's "Two Forces." This angle is 2° less than that assigned by Camper to his Kalmuck and Negro. In Tenniel's "The Fenian-Pest" (21 February 1866), a title chosen to evoke the rinderpest then ravaging English livestock, the figure of Britannia has a profile of some 75°, in contrast to 47° for the Fenian.[92] And in "Two Forces," already cited, Britannia received an angle of 92°, or 24° more than that given to the Fenian stereotype. Matt Morgan's ape-like figure in "The Irish Frankenstein" cannot be properly measured because his face has not been drawn in profile, but the angle cannot possibly be much higher than 50°, whereas Dr. Frankenstein has a fine Anglo-Saxon angle of some 80°.[93] Returning to Tenniel's cartoons in *Punch* for the sake of comparison, we find Lord John Russell with a facial angle of 87° (5 September 1863), Gladstone with angles of 85° and 87° (11 May 1867 and 19 November 1881), and Disraeli with a less flattering angle of 74° (23 February 1867).[94] Moving farther afield but not far away in time, we encounter Sidney Paget who made the features of Sherlock Holmes familiar to thousands of *Strand* readers. Paget's famous profiles of Holmes range from roughly 72° to 86°, the average of five such measurements being 78°. Across the Atlantic, the American illustrator of *The Adventures of Sherlock Holmes*, Frederick Dorr Steele, endowed the detective with an even higher average of 85°, based on ten measurements.[95] In sum, the Anglo-Saxon ideal type of the later nineteenth century had a facial angle between the high seventies and the high eighties, but the same artists and illustrators assigned angles in the fifties and sixties to Irish Fenians and Land Leaguers. These lower facial angles placed politicized Paddy in much the same company as the orangutan and the gorilla.

The close correspondence between facial angles and character or behavioral traits in Victorian caricature was no accident or coincidence. The comic artists who delighted in turning men into facsimiles of apes and angels had all picked up the rudiments of anatomy and a rough idea of Camper's system in their early training or apprenticeship. Whether unconsciously or not, virtually all Victorian cartoonists and caricaturists relied on the facial angle as a means of epitomizing character. The equating of high facial angles with such qualities as beauty, strength, valor, integrity, and moral rectitude endures to this day, as does the converse equation of low facial angles with undesirable qualities in human beings. Those artists who draw comic strips and comic books for children of all ages employ as wide a range of facial angles as did their Victorian predecessors. The creators of the crime and adventure serials in what are inappropriately called "comic" books consistently award high facial angles to their "all-American" heroes, whose physiognomies derive from the Victorian ideal of the "Greek gods," so intensely cultivated in English public schools; and these same comic artists tend to assign angles less than 75° to their villains, many of whose features betray a distinctly Sicilian, not Roman, ancestry. In a comic coloring book published several years ago, for example, Superboy was given a facial angle ranging between 81° and 87°, and his father, who came from a super-civilization in outer space, bore a lofty angle of 90°. To complete this fantasy and to heighten the superiority of this ideal type, the artists at Jason Studios gave Superboy's high school teacher a mortal angle of 76° along with a slightly sinister pencil moustache.[96]

The criterion of the facial angle ought not to be applied indiscriminately to all cartoons and caricatures regardless of subject and time. It works best as a rough gauge of the artists' intentions, when the artists themselves were trained in a tradition of which Camperian lore was a part and subscribed to the theory that the degree of orthognathism and prognathism in the human face was a fairly reliable guide to the worth or value of an individual. Some of the more politicized artists of the thermonuclear age have broken completely with Victorian conventions of physiognomy, and these men have done far greater violence to the physical features of man than was ever contemplated by Tenniel and his school. The grotesque distortions of the human face achieved by such caricaturists as Gerald Scarfe and David Levine, both of whom excell at the art of making the faces of politicians and statesmen look obscene, are a radical departure from the adherence of Victorian cartoonists to the facial angle. To attempt to apply Camper's angle to the productions of Scarfe and Levine would be not only futile, but an admission that one had missed their point.

The simianization of Paddy by some Victorian comic artists was a serious preoccupation which had important social and political ramifications so far as the Irish people in the British Isles and overseas were concerned. But there were moments when an almost farcical note entered the picture. After all, these cartoonists were by repute, if not by temperament, men of wit and insight who enjoyed a good laugh at the foibles of their fellow human beings. On at least one occasion that laughter lost some of its edge. A prolific contributor to *Punch* in the years 1880–94 was Harry Furniss, an extremely versatile and gifted comic artist.[97] Although Furniss loved to play games with his pen, often filling a drawing with artfully hidden faces, he was also an acute satirist of the political arena. Shortly after joining the artists' staff at *Punch*, he was invited by the well-known journalist, Henry W. Lucy, who was deservedly known as "the Pepys of Parliament," to illustrate his special

21 *"Swift MacNeill Refuses to be Named."* The caricature that caused a row at Westminster. Harry Furniss of *Punch* simianizes John G. Swift MacNeill, the Irish nationalist member of Parliament in the act of denying any disorderly conduct during a heated debate in the House of Commons in August 1893. (*Punch*, 26 August 1893.)

54

series in that weekly, called "The Essence of Parliament—Extracted from the Diary of Toby, M.P." For a number of years these two men produced a popular commentary, full of barbed allusions and innuendoes in prose and cartoon, on the week's events at Westminster. The Irish parliamentary party, so well drilled and ably led by Parnell, became one of the favorite targets of Furniss's pen, and Irish nationalists loved him none the more because he had been born in Ireland of an Anglo-Scottish marriage. During the Home Rule debates of 1886 and 1893, Furniss conveyed his strong Unionist sentiments through an assortment of cartoons, large and small, all of them depicting the Parnellites and, after 1891, the anti-Parnellites too, as a gang of hooligans given to unruly behavior in the House of Commons. The more militant the posture of the Irish nationalists at Westminster became, the more wild-eyed and siminian featured were his caricatures of Parnell's party. By the summer of 1893, in the midst of the crucial debate on the second Home Rule Bill, Furniss's barbs had worked their way well into the flanks of his Irish victims.

On 26 August 1893, *Punch* carried a small drawing of the member of Parliament for South Donegal, the flamboyant J. G. Swift MacNeill, who had recently denied in the House of Commons having made any unparliamentary remarks about an Unionist speaker during a particularly disorderly debate. Furniss made his sketch of Swift MacNeill look as much like an ape as was possible without distorting the features out of all recognition, and the facial angle was a mere 61°.[98] This drawing was too much for the volatile MacNeill to bear, and he made plans with some of his Irish colleagues to teach the artist better manners. Led by MacNeill, a small posse of Irish nationalist members of Parliament waylaid Furniss in the lobby of the House of Commons and proceeded to berate him with the richest epithets at their command. Still highly indignant at being caricatured in such "an exuberant and unflattering" way, MacNeill lost his temper and committed a "technical assault" on the artist. Dr. Tanner and several other nationalists contributed their share of verbal violence. Furniss wisely avoided a physical response, not just because he was outnumbered but also because he realized that the Irish members wanted to goad him into an altercation that would end with his being excluded from the lobby of the House where he earned his livelihood. So he withdrew from this skirmish shaken and somewhat the wiser.[99]

It did not take Furniss long to work out his revenge. On 9 September there appeared a small filler in the columns of *Punch* which ran as follows: "No Doubt of It.—Of course the admission detracts from our 'Lika Joko's' artistic skill, but evidently Mr. Swift-to-Avenge MacNeill is a person very easily 'drawn.'"[100] "Lika Joko" was the signature Furniss often used for his comic sketches in "The Diary of Toby, M.P." and also for his stylized drawings called "Japanneries." Two weeks later, on 23 September, *Punch* carried a full-page cartoon of a scene in the House of Commons wherein the Irish parliamentary party and their Liberal allies were endowed with the most sublime and beautiful faces. In the foreground stood Swift MacNeill restored to human form with a facial angle of 78° and wearing a most angelic expression. Crouching in the bottom left-hand corner was the figure of an ape holding pen and sketch pad: a self-portrait of the artist as a diminuitive simian with a facial angle of 67°. The title of this drawing, which was signed "Lika Joko," was only too appropriate: "A House of Apollo-ticians—As Seen by Themselves."[101] Furniss thus succeeded in turning both his own cheek and the tables on his foes. According to the historian of *Punch*, Furniss added the following piece of doggerel to this cartoon:

O, Mr. MacNeill was quite happy until a
Draughtsman in *Punch* made him like a gorilla—
At the Zoo the gorilla quite happy did feel
Till the draughtsman in *Punch* made him like the MacNeill.[102]

22 *"A House of Apollo-ticians—As Seen by Themselves."* Harry Furniss turns Swift MacNeill and his fellow Home Rulers into near-angels, after being physically abused by some Irish nationalists in the lobby of the House of Commons. The cartoonist has reduced himself to simian stature in the lower left-hand corner to complete the effect of this reversal of images. (*Punch*, 23 September 1893.)

What better example could there be of the ability of caricature to provoke, and the power of the caricaturist to parry as well as to parody the thrust of his victims?

Punch's penchant for poking fun at Paddy or "happy-go-lucky Pat" continued well into the present century: witness the little anthology of cartoons and jokes on Irish subjects which appeared in the series, *Punch Library of Humour*. Entitled *Mr. Punch's Irish Humour*, this volume is crammed with Paddy figures drawn by Charles Keene, Phil May, and other comic artists of the late Victorian era. Although none of Tenniel's Fenian ape-men appear in this "delightful collection of Irish wit and high spirits," the title page contains a sketch of a simianized Paddy (facial angle, 70°); and the first full-page cartoon thereafter (page 9) depicts "Mr. MacSimius," a heavily bewhiskered, albeit relatively orthognathous Irishman, proclaiming to the world: "Well, Oi don't profess to be a particularly cultivated man meself; but at laste me progenitors were all educated in the hoigher branches!" Although unsigned, this cartoon resembles the style of another Scottish artist, George Denholm Armour, born in 1864, who studied at the Royal Scottish Academy before emigrating to London in 1888.

Even before the outbreak of World War I, however, English cartoonists were losing their appetite for simianized Paddies, and they returned to such traditional symbols as Erin or Hibernia, the "Distressful Damsel," and the inevitable Irish pig. By 1914, the "gorilla controversy" had lost its cutting edge or, rather, its ability to wound the *amour propre* of God-fearing Englishmen. *Punch's* artists gradually restored human features to Irish Celts, and even ardent Sinn Feiners were let off lightly with moderate mid-facial prognathism. The ape-like Irishman did make a fleeting reappearance in *Punch* in the early 1920s during the bitter guerrilla war fought by Sinn Fein militants against the forces of the Crown. In his feature cartoon, "A Midsummer Nightmare" (23 June 1920), L. Raven-Hill used the old Tenniel formula on a shadowy Irish face in order to show what kind of brute John Bull had to deal with in Ireland. The lesser known artist A. W. Lloyd produced a simianized Irishman, representing the Irish Republican Army, in a small cartoon (27 October 1920). But these were the only two examples of that almost extinct species, the Irish gorilla, in the entire year's output. More typical of *Punch's* postwar attitude to Ireland was the work of Bernard Partridge, the principal cartoonist of that era. In his "The Great Postponement" (24 December 1919), "A Test of Sagacity" (18 February 1920), and "The Experts" (13 October 1920), Partridge used the pig to denote the Irish people; and the poignant figure of fair Erin dominated several other feature cartoons, among them "A Session of Common Sense" (1 September 1920) and "The Promise of Rain on a Parched Land" (13 July 1921). In the world of English comic art, the hardy pig outlived both Paddy and the gorilla as the representative of the Irish people.

57

CHAPTER V   # Irish-American Apes

THE RELIANCE OF SOME ENGLISH CARICATURISTS on the simian and bestial idiom to epitomize Irish character in the age of the Fenians and the Land League invites a brief comparison with the work of some leading American comic artists and illustrators in the same period. Since there are many points of comparability, it may be best to begin with the most famous of America's caricaturists in the later nineteenth century, Thomas Nast (1840–1902). Because Nast was born in the German Palatinate, one might suspect that in an ethnocentric age his Teutonic heritage would predispose him to feel contempt toward such inferior breeds as the Irish Celts of America. But it is far more likely that his unflattering cartoons of Irish-Americans derived from his wish to root out corruption, bossism, and racial as well as religious (i.e., Irish Catholic) bigotry from American society. In more than one respect, Nast was a product of European dissent in 1848. Transplanted to America, he became a radical Republican and moderate Protestant who deplored the iniquities of the Tweed ring and Tammany Hall and lampooned the white supremacists of postbellum America.[103] In 1860 he spent some months in London while on assignment to cover the Italian wars of unification, and it was then that he met Tenniel whose work he greatly admired. Upon his return to America, he joined *Harper's Weekly* with which he had a long and formative association. Nast saw few redeeming features in those Irish-American politicians who formed a powerful bloc in the Democratic party, especially in the New York area, and who were as intolerant of Negroes as they were insistent on parochial schooling at public expense. Whenever Nast drew an Irish-American, he invariably produced a *lusus naturae* or cross between a professional boxer and an orangutan. The degree of midfacial prognathism and the size of the mouth have to be seen to be believed.

Simianized Irish-Americans inhabit many of Nast's cartoons in *Harper's Weekly*, including "The Day We Celebrate: St. Patrick's Day, 1867" (6 April 1867), "Shadows of Forthcoming Events" (22 January 1870), and "Our Modern Falstaff Reviewing his Army" (5 November 1870).[104] The repulsive features of the Irish-American in "The Ignorant Vote—Honors Are Easy" (9 December 1876) corresponded with English versions of Fenian Paddy; but there is at least one vital difference. Nast gave his Irish-born brute an abnormally high facial angle of 87°, compared with 70° for the Negro facing him on the scales.[105] Perhaps Nast considered this epitome of "white trash"

23 *"The Day We Celebrate: St. Patrick's Day, 1867."* Thomas Nast celebrates the stereotypical Irish-American street fight or "shindy" with this stirring scene of simianized Celts beating respectable citizens and the police in New York City. (*Harper's Weekly*, 6 April 1867.)

more American than Irish. In any event, the 17° difference between the two faces is not without significance.

American cartoonists on the whole tended to endow their Irish-American stereotypes with squarer jaws, stronger chins, and higher facial angles than did their English counterparts. Sherlock Holmes's features underwent the same "face-lift" in America, as we have already seen, and one is reminded of Dick Tracy's enormous jaw—a case of Irish-American chin preeminence—which survives in a comic strip to this day. Whether this tendency to higher facial angles and stronger chins may be construed as a sign of greater toleration toward Irish Celts in America than in England is a debatable matter. New York's leading cartoonists of the 1870s and 1880s certainly did not refrain from simianizing Irish-American Paddies who epitomized the tens of thousands of working-class immigrants and their children caught up in urban poverty and slum conditions after their flight from rural poverty and famine in Ireland.

Much the same formula for degrading Irish features was used in two comic weeklies published in New York, namely, *Puck* and *Judge*. The

HARPER'S WEEKLY.

A JOURNAL OF CIVILIZATION

Vol. XX.—No. 1041.]   NEW YORK, SATURDAY, DECEMBER 9, 1876.   [WITH A SUPPLEMENT. PRICE TEN CENTS.

Entered according to Act of Congress, in the Year 1876, by Harper & Brothers, in the Office of the Librarian of Congress, at Washington.

THE IGNORANT VOTE—HONORS ARE EASY.

24   *"The Ignorant Vote: Honors Are Easy."* Nast depicts the balance of political forces in America during Reconstruction with this cartoon of emancipated slaves in the south carrying as much weight as the nasty, brutish, and simian Irish-American voter in the north. The proverbial clay pipe in his hatband reinforces the "White's" ethnicity. (*Harper's Weekly*, 9 December 1876.)

60

25 *Paddy Aping Uncle Sam.* In this detail from Joseph Keppler's "Under False Colors," the wild Irish-American Paddy is being exposed by the American authorities as a prognathous dynamiter serving the cause of Irish freedom and anarchy rather than that of law and order in America. (From *Puck*, volume 11, number 263, 22 March 1882, pages 40–41.)

founder and driving force behind *Puck* was Joseph Keppler (1838–94), the son of a Viennese confectioner who had fled to America in 1848.[106] Keppler was reared in Vienna where he studied art before emigrating to America in 1867. After several false starts in journalism in St. Louis's German community, Keppler went to New York in 1873 to work for *Frank Leslie's Illustrated Newspaper*. Three years later he decided to revive a German-language comic weekly he had once produced called *Puck*. Backed by a close friend, A. Schwartzmann, *Puck* proved such a success that Keppler started an English-language edition in 1877. This new *Puck* was one of the first American comic weeklies to use chromolithography to effect, and the periodical enjoyed a good run, lasting until 1918. Unlike most English comic weeklies *Puck* carried three handsome color cartoons in each number, in addition to various black-and-white illustrations. The Austrian flavor of *Puck* was reinforced by several artists whom Keppler imported from Vienna. But *Puck* also employed several first-rate American cartoonists, among whom James Albert Wales (1852–86) merits special mention.

Wales started out as a wood engraver in Toledo, Ohio, before moving to New York in 1873. He was another of those migratory cartoonists who hopped from one weekly to another, never fully satisfied with his immediate situation. After working briefly for *Frank Leslie's Illustrated Newspaper*, he traveled to London in 1875 where he landed jobs with *Judy* and *The Illustrated Sporting and Dramatic News*. He returned to work for Frank Leslie in 1877, but soon joined *Puck* where he stayed until 1881. Wales left in that year to become cartoonist of *Puck's* new rival, *Judge*, which had been launched by W. J. Arkell. In 1885 Wales went back to *Puck*, being unhappy with editorial policies at *Judge*, and he remained there until his untimely death in the following year.[107]

Another talented member of *Puck's* staff for a time was Bernhard Gillam (1856–96), who was born in Banbury, England, the seventh of fourteen children. In 1866 he moved with his family to New York where he received only the rudiments of an education. In the late 1870s he began to draw for *Frank Leslie's Illustrated Newspaper*, that haven for emigré artists, and also for the *New York Graphic*. After a brief association with Nast on *Harper's Weekly*, he joined the staff of *Puck* from 1881 to 1886, when he left to become part owner and director of *Judge* which up to that time had been owned and managed by his brother-in-law Arkell. For ten years Gillam guided *Judge* until it had attained a position of national eminence in the realm of political cartoons.[108] With a few exceptions New York's comic weeklies were a good deal more partisan in their politics than those in London, and American cartoonists tended to treat political figures, whether local or national, to much more scathing ridicule than was usual in England.

There are so many splendid examples of the simianized Irish-American in *Puck* and *Judge* that it is hard to decide which ones deserve mention and which of those deserve to be reproduced if only in black and white. Some of

26 *Prognathism in Ireland.* Frederick B. Opper's drawing of Paddy and his wife
in their native habitat, entitled "The King of A-Shantee," reinforces the ties
between Irish Celts and Black Africans by playing on the word Ashanti, while
Paddy's simian features suggest the "missing link." (From *Puck*, volume 10, number 258, 15 February 1882, page 378.)

27 *"The Irish Skirmishers' 'Blind Pool'."* This cartoon by Frederick B. Opper stresses the gullibility as well as prognathism of those Irish immigrants who were foolish enough to donate their hard-earned dollars to the Skirmishing Fund, allegedly run by and for unscrupulous politicians. (From *Puck*, volume 12, number 287, 6 September 1882, page 16.)

Keppler's finest Paddies appeared in 1882, among them being "Under False Colors," "Uncle Sam's Lodging-House," and "British Benevolence."[109] Two other cartoonists who worked for *Puck* in the 1880s, Frederick B. Opper and F. Grätz, also excelled at simianizing Irish-Americans. Wales drew some memorable Irish gorillas in his feature cartoons, including "Pat Puzzled —'Co-er-cion—Phwat's That?'" and "A St. Patrick's Day Vision" which appeared in *Puck* (16 February and 16 March 1881 respectively).[110] And Gillam took his simianized Irish Celts with him from *Puck* to *Judge*. The simile of the simian Celt thus crossed the Atlantic, gaining a higher facial angle and a bigger, squarer jaw en route, and became as closely identified with corruption, clericalism, and organized violence in America as in the British Isles. The leading cartoonists of New York in this period used much the same physiognomical device as Tenniel, Proctor, and Bowcher in order to convey attitudes about the essence of Irish character which were widely held in both countries. However different the politics of Tenniel and Nast,

28 *"American Gold."* Frederick B. Opper drew these stereotypes of Irish Celtic simianism in the New World and the Old for *Puck.* Note the suggestion that the "gold" earned by menial labor in New York fell into the hands of professional politicians or agitators rather than into the laps of idle, improvident relatives in Ireland. (From *Puck,* volume 11, number 272, 24 May 1882, page 194.)

both men regarded the politicized Irish Celt as a menace to the good society which they wished respectively to preserve and achieve.

In spite of their fondness of the simian simile, the cartoonists of *Puck* and *Judge* were not blind to the existence of decent and even human qualities in many Irishmen. Like their English counterparts, these comic artists represented the soul of Ireland as a beautiful, dark-haired, and wide-eyed woman, usually labeled Erin or Hibernia. This sorrowful and irresistible paragon of Irish womanhood, who was always being threatened or abused by some monster, was the one symbol on which the cartoonists of London, Dublin, and New York were wholly agreed. Some of New York's cartoonists, in particular Gillam, occasionally drew handsome Irish faces when they wanted to depict the fate of evicted tenants and innocent victims of agrarian outrage in Ireland. Although some effort was made to discriminate between good and bad Irish Celts, it is fair to say that the politicized apes far outnumbered the apolitical angels.

65

29 *The Simian Irish Celt.* In this *Puck* cartoon of "An Irish Jig" by James A. Wales, both John Bull and Uncle Sam despair of being able to tame the wild Irish Celt, grown fat on the larders of England and America—including drugs—by peaceful methods. (From *Puck*, volume 8, number 191, 3 November 1880, page 150.)

30 *The Simian Irish Celt.* In this detail from James A. Wales' "An Irish Jig," the
marked similarities between the caricaturist's stereotypes of Paddy and orangutans and chimpanzees may be seen. (From *Puck*, volume 8, number 191, 3
November 1880, page 150.)

CHAPTER VI   # Irish Angels

THE STEREOTYPE OF SIMIAN PADDY may have fetched a good price in the cartoonists' market along Fleet Street and the Strand, but in Ireland, home of the alleged Calibans and ape-men, this image was effectively reversed. Dublin's cartoonists, for example, invariably represented Irish tenant farmers and their elected leaders as angels, albeit lacking halos and wings. Those comic weeklies and monthlies which sought to amuse Ireland's urban middle- and upper-middle classes between 1870 and 1914 employed artists and illustrators who were accustomed to drawing their countrymen as handsome, sturdy, honest human beings, and even though they made no systematic effort to simianize their political opponents, these cartoonists knew how to make John Bull's officials or minions in Ireland look like brutes with huge jaws and cruel faces. The average life span of Dublin's comic weeklies was less than two years, and even then it required strict management and renewed subsidies to keep them going. Unfortunately, little is known about the artists and writers who worked for these periodicals, and details about their circulation and finances are more than scarce.[111] In most cases, these humorous reviews were owned as well as published by established printing firms in Dublin which could afford to sustain at least one unprofitable venture on the strength of their income from commercial printing and allied activities.

Dublin's comic weeklies and monthlies were aimed at a primarily urban audience, made up of the professional and propertied classes with some leisure and a desire for less serious and less political reading matter than was to be found in the newspapers. The comic relief in question usually consisted of corny and clean Paddy jokes, overworked Irish bulls, satirical comment and cartoons on both municipal and national politics, and columns of unadulterated gossip. Although much of their material concerned Dublin society alone, most of the editors kept a close watch on London's comic weeklies, and all of them aspired to produce something as successful as *Punch*.

The first Dublin periodical to make a serious bid for the title of the Irish *Punch* was *Zozimus*, a one-penny weekly which was launched in May 1870 and lasted until August 1872. Named after the legendary blind poet and wise man, *Zozimus* employed an artist named John Fergus O'Hea (1850–1922), who deserves to rank among the finest political cartoonists of the Victorian era. Often signing himself "Spex," O'Hea became a master of the color cartoon, and his career of over forty-five years was certainly more variegated than that of Tenniel.[112] O'Hea also illustrated several books and drew a number of pictures depicting "great moments" in the Irish struggle against the Saxon yoke.[113] Some of his poster-size lithographs appeared in the Christmas numbers of such literary magazines as *Young Ireland*, *The Sunshine*, and *The Irish Fireside*, and they were as rich in color as in detail. Unfortunately, O'Hea's skills as an illustrator and cartoonist have been unrecognized by the compilers of the standard reference works on Victorian art, so that information about him is fragmentary. After the demise of *Zozimus* in 1872, he worked his way through many of Dublin's leading comic weeklies, including *Zoz* (1876–78), *Pat* (1879–83), *Ireland's Eye* (1874–82?), and *The Irish Figaro* (1898–1901). During the 1880s he also drew the color supplement for *The Weekly Freeman*; and toward the end of his career, in 1914–15, he drew cartoons for both *The Lepracaun* and *The Quiz* (1915).

O'Hea was a serious political cartoonist with pronounced Home Rule convictions, and he promoted the Parnellite cause with both skill and perseverance. Like all of Dublin's nationalist cartoonists, O'Hea liked to make Home Rulers look not only human, but handsome and trustworthy in his cartoons. The Pat of his imagination was an ideal type with a high facial angle and regular features completely devoid of any midfacial prognathism and "peasant" expression. While preferring to beautify the faces of his national heroes, O'Hea enjoyed making Orangemen, policemen, emergency men who helped to evict tenants, and the officials of Dublin Castle look as ugly and brutish as possible. In "The European Civiliser" which appeared in *Zozimus* on 8 June 1870, he produced a repugnant English stereotype called "Bill Stiggins of Uxbridge," who was a huge masher with muscular face, broken nose, and protruding lower jaw. This powerful brute is shown conniving with a bloodthirsty Balkan who stands on ground strewn with the bodies of his innocent victims.[114]

After *Zozimus* folded in 1872, O'Hea worked as a free-lancer for several years before joining the staff of *Zoz* in 1876. Edited by Edwin Hamilton, who had won the vice-chancellor's prize at Trinity College, Dublin, with a humorous poem, *Zoz* lasted half the distance of its precursor. In hopes of expanding the circulation, O'Hea and his fellow cartoonists, John D. Reigh and A. F. Blood, were asked to play down national politics and to play up Dublin society and aldermanic personalities in their work. *Zoz* was much less aggressively Home Rule in outlook than *Zozimus*, but even this change of pace did not guarantee success, and *Zoz* folded in 1877. The combination of Hamilton and O'Hea reappeared several years later with the launching of *Pat*, a three-penny comic weekly, in December 1879. Describing itself as "An Irish Weekly Periodical; Artistic, Literary, Humorous, Satirical," *Pat* was owned and printed by the firm of Tomsohn and Wogan which specialized in chromolithography, engraving, printing, and design.

31 "*Reciprocity.*" An Irish cartoonist reverses English images in *Pat*. John F. O'Hea creates a suitable stereotype for "the representative Englishman," on the right, to accompany the simianized Paddy of London's comic weeklies. (*Pat*, 7 February 1880.)

No. 1.—This is little Chalks sent over by the London Illustrated Smudge to furnish truthful sketches of Irish character.

No. 2.—This is his model.

No. 3.—And this is the sketch he furnishes.

32 *"Setting Down in Malice."* The cartoonist of *Pat*, possibly John F. O'Hea, mocks the habitual distortion of Irish facial features by London's artists in their attempt to please their English readers. (*Pat*, new series, volume 1, number 2, 22 January 1881.)

Pat's Home Rule sympathies were often buried in a welter of light verse and heavy-handed humor. O'Hea's cover figure of a puckish Pat with kindly eyes and grin betrayed no signs of prognathism. Among the comic bric-a-brac of this periodical was a special column called "Pat's Diary," written in a stage-Irish brogue that would have made the Irish-American author of "Mr. Dooley" wince. O'Hea's version of Pat the tenant farmer was a good-looking and good-natured man with only a touch of chin prominence. In some of his cartoons dealing with the Home Rule movement, he neatly reversed the simianizing process of London's comic artists by drawing English ape-men with the object of showing how easily two could play this game. In his amusing cartoon, "Reciprocity," O'Hea juxtaposed the simianized Irish Paddy of Fleet Street with the equally distorted figure of "the representative Englishman" whose facial features matched his black-jack and crowbar.[115] O'Hea struck an even more telling blow against English stereotypes of the Irish in his "Setting Down In Malice," which appeared in *Pat* on 22 January 1881. Here, he used only three small sketches to expose the nature of the simianizing process. This graphic story of an English cartoonist who goes to Ireland in search of Celtic realities, finds a handsome Irishman, and then deliberately caricatures him as a vicious gorilla conveys the mechanics of stereotyping far more effectively than words.

O'Hea occasionally reversed the simian image in a more direct manner, as may be seen in his sketch of a scene in the House of Commons, wherein an angelic Irish Home Ruler is being set upon and gagged by several ape-like English and Scottish members of Parliament, including "The McAss, M.P. for Haggis."[116] At the end of September 1880, *Pat* succumbed tempor-arily to an internal crisis, and after several months' absence, a resuscitated *Pat* reached the newsstands in January 1881. Costing one penny and wear-ing a different cover, the new *Pat* was produced by W. P. Swan at the Carlton Steam Printing Works. Although the feature cartoons remained unsigned, O'Hea presumably continued on the staff, but this time he had the assistance of a promising young cartoonist, Thomas Fitzpatrick (1860–1912). The artistic skills of O'Hea and Fitzpatrick combined to make *Pat* a stimulating weekly until its collapse for financial reasons in March 1883. In a number of fine color cartoons, O'Hea hammered home the failures of Liberal policy in Ireland and the necessity of both legislative and economic independence from England. Some of his most effective cartoons contrasted handsome and reliable Pat with unscrupulous English politicians at West-minster bidding for the Irish vote. Other cartoons mocked the English habit of exaggerating Irish agrarian crime out of all recognition so as to blacken Irish character, and showed how cruelly Irish landlords oppressed their tenants. O'Hea thus proved beyond any doubt that Irish cartoonists could fight English apes with Irish angels and carry on the Home Rule campaign more effectively in color than in black and white.

A Dublin penny weekly with some unusual qualities was *The Jarvey*, which lasted from 3 January 1889 to 27 December 1890. This periodical was the first editorial venture of William Percy French (1854–1920), the versatile humorist, poet, parodist, songwriter, watercolorist, and entertainer. Percy French came from a well-known Anglo-Irish family in County Roscommon, and by his own account he remained "the small boy messing about with a paintbox, or amusing myself with pencil and paper" all his life. After taking a leisurely degree at Trinity College, Dublin, he dabbled briefly in engineering and then worked as an inspector for the Board of Works in County Cavan before taking up the serious work of being a humorist. As a supplement to his meager salary, French contributed occasional articles to a popular journal, *The Irish Cyclist*, which was edited and published by R. J. Mecredy. When French lost his job at the Board of Works through a cutback in staff, he asked Mecredy for a regular position on *The Irish Cyclist*. Mecredy suggested instead that he edit a new comic weekly, and French thus became editor and chief contributor of *The Jarvey*. Through strenuous efforts he kept this unprofitable weekly alive for almost two years, resorting to bad puns and farfetched prize competitions in a vain attempt to boost sales. A reviewer in the *Freeman's Journal* delivered this solemn verdict on the new weekly: "We have before us the first number of a journal devoted to art and humour. Some of the jokes we've seen before—some we haven't seen yet."[117] *The Jarvey's* chief cartoonist was Richard Caulfeild Orpen, a close friend of French, who also belonged to an Anglo-Irish landowning family of some distinction, the Orpens of Stillorgan, County Dublin. Richard later became a successful architect, but his chief claim to fame today derives from his youngest brother, the eminent portrait painter, Sir William Orpen (1878–1931). Percy French teamed with Dick Orpen to produce not only *The Jarvey* but several light-hearted asides such as *Racquetry Rhymes* (Dublin, 1888), a satire on the new craze for tennis, and *The First Lord Liftinant* (Dublin, 1890). They filled the pages of *The Jarvey* with a "gentrified" humor, all of which was fit to print if not to read. Eschewing politics as much as possible, they concentrated on jokes about life in Irish castles and cabins; and when the weekly failed at the end of 1890, French observed how strange it was that in a country "famous the world over for its wit and humour, no comic paper has the remotest chance of even paying its way."[118]

Dick Orpen was not insensitive to the image of Irishmen drawn by English cartoonists, and in one of his rare political cartoons he took up the cudgel already wielded by O'Hea. In his "Mr. Punch Introduces Tenniel's Irishman to The Jarvey," reproduced here, we see the pensive, orthognathous "Jarvey" looking at the prognathous brute drawn by Tenniel from "hearsay," and then declaring that monsters like this one might be found in Whitechapel, but not in Ireland.[119] Because Orpen did not belong to the same social class as O'Hea and Fitzpatrick, he was quite capable of drawing the occasional prognathous Paddy, and some of his small drawings for such regular columns in *The Jarvey* as "Carmen Eblanae," "Tail Ends of Mane Events," and the

33 "*Mr. Punch Introduces Tenniel's Irishman to The Jarvey.*" Richard C. Orpen,
cartoonist for *The Jarvey*, shows Mr. Jarvey's skeptical reaction to the simianized
wild Irishman drawn by Tenniel in *Punch*. (From *The Jarvey*, 9 February 1889.)

reveries of Flanagan the poet betray marked midfacial prognathism as well as chin prominence, however far removed these faces may be from the Calibans and Frankenstein monsters of Tenniel and Morgan. Orpen was content to perpetuate the older image of Paddy as a slow-witted and primitive purveyor of Irish bulls. If he drew some Paddies from an Anglo-Irish point of view, he also liked to distort Negroid features in the approved Victorian manner, when mocking certain aspects of American life.

Apart from Orpen, whose background and fleeting career as a cartoonist make him something of an exception in the world of Dublin's comic artists, there was only one Dubliner in the 1880s who refused to beautify or "angelicize" Pat the stereotypical Irish farmer. This was Richard Thomas Moynan (1856–1906) who signed most of his work as "Lex," which was an appropriate choice for the principal cartoonist of *The Unionist*, a militantly Tory newspaper published weekly in Dublin.[120] Moynan was a mediocre artist, but he was still enough of an Irishman to avoid any indulgence in the simian device, and his drawings for *The Unionist* concentrated more on political issues and events than on physiognomies and facial angles.

For more than half a century, from the 1860s to World War I, Dublin's cartoonists observed the convention of Erin and Pat, those two figures of beauty and integrity which occupied a special place in nationalist symbolism. Erin was a stately as well as sad and wise woman, usually drawn in flowing robes, embroidered with shamrocks. Her hair was long and dark, falling well down her back; her eyes were round and melancholy, set in a face of flawless symmetry. Occasionally she wore a garland of shamrocks and appeared with a harp and an Irish wolfhound in the foreground. Erin suggested all that was feminine, courageous, and chaste about Irish womanhood, and she made an ideal Andromeda waiting to be rescued by a suitable Perseus. As we have seen, this figure of Erin, which was far more feminine than the virago known as Britannia, was the one symbol on which the cartoonists of London, Dublin, and New York were in more or less complete agreement.[121]

Erin's complementary companion was Pat who was the epitome of Irish masculinity. His face was long but full, his forehead high, his chin square, and his nose and mouth straight and firm. There was a twinkle in his eyes and an easygoing smile, marking him as a man prepared to trust anyone of equal good faith. Pat was no landless laborer or cottier peasant. His clothes and bearing signified a respectable tenant who farmed upwards of fifteen or twenty acres. A far cry from the mid-Victorian Paddy of English imaginations, Pat was hardheaded and not likely to be fooled by calculating politicians, devious land agents, or harsh landlords. O'Hea's version of Pat possessed a fine facial angle in the low 80s, and the well-proportioned features gave the impression of a man who was not only ready but anxious to manage his own affairs.

During the 1880s, when the Irish parliamentary party was in its prime and relatively free from factional fights, Dublin's cartoonists tended to draw the Parnellites as though they were angels on earth. In *Pat, The Irish Pilot Ireland's Eye, The Sunshine,* and *The Jarvey,* the agents of the Irish nationalist struggle against British rule, landlordism, and Protestant bigotry were endowed with handsome, orthognathous faces. At general-election time, cartoonists such as O'Hea and Reigh drew special supplements for the leading newspapers which contained flattering portraits of the nationalist candidates.[122] After the fall of Parnell in 1891, however, these same artists focused attention on the fierce factionalism that ensued, and the faces of the Parnellite and anti-Parnellite leaders began to look less attractive when drawn by cartoonists who belonged to the rival camp. Parnell's features, on the other hand, were generally spared serious distortion, and in both London and Dublin the "uncrowned king" received far better treatment in cartoons than any of his devoted followers.

By the early 1880s, most of Dublin's largest newspapers had started to publish weekly color cartoons which were printed on separate sheets and folded inside the Saturday edition. These special supplements varied in size even within the same year,[123] but they were all chromolithographs with an increasingly effective range of colors being used. Devoted in the main to the Home Rule movement and the agrarian question, these color cartoons maintained a high standard of draughtsmanship and artistry. If one were to collate the weekly supplements drawn by J. D. Reigh for *United Ireland;* by O'Hea, Fitzpatrick, Phil Blake, W. C. Mills, and W. T. O'Shea for *The Weekly Freeman* (after 1892, *The Weekly Freeman and National Press*); and by the unknown artists of *The Weekly News* as well as *The Irish Times;* the result would be a fascinating montage of Irish political life in the generation before World War I.

These color cartoons repeated the same message already encountered in some of Dublin's comic weeklies and monthlies: the forces of good represented by Erin, Pat, and the Parnellites, were confronting the forces of evil represented by Dublin Castle, the apparatus of coercion, evicting landlords, Orangemen, and fair-weather patriots. About the outcome of that contest there could be little doubt, even though the fulfillment of Erin's dream of a united, independent Ireland was usually drawn in near the horizon. Even the supplements of *The Weekly Irish Times,* a paper known for its Unionist leanings, contained rather handsome Parnellites in spite of the editor's disapproval of the Land League. The prognathous features in all of these supplements belong to the agents of Dublin Castle and Orangemen.[124] Occasionally John Bull as well as the British working-class stereotype, in particular the Birmingham supporters of Joseph Chamberlain, came in for their share of face-lowering in these cartoons.[125] Most of Dublin's cartoonists delighted in distorting the features of those whom they considered responsible for Ireland's ills, and during the era of Liberal as well as Tory repression in the 1880s, both the Earl of Spencer, Lord Lieutenant from 1882 to 1885, and Arthur Balfour, Chief Secretary from 1887 to 1891, became ghoulish, prancing sadists in the weekly supplements. No sooner had Lord Spencer agreed to serve in Gladstone's Home Rule ministry of 1886, however, than these same cartoonists began to soften his features and restore him to the ranks of civilized physiognomies. Balfour, being the first Chief Secretary in living memory to carry through a policy of stringent coercion and to emerge at the end not only in good health but with a greatly enhanced political reputation, remained the fiendish jailer and would-be executioner in the eyes of these Home Rule cartoonists.

Some of the most effective of the weekly supplements were drawn by Thomas Fitzpatrick, who deserves a place alongside O'Hea and John Reigh as Dublin's best political cartoonists during the Home Rule period. "Fitz" was born in Cork in 1860 and as a youth he became an apprentice litho-grapher in a large printing firm there. After moving to Dublin where he worked for *Pat* in the early 1880s, he left for London in the hope of improv-ing his fortunes. Several years of ups and downs spurred him to return to Dublin, and he then branched out into design and photoengraving. Later on he began to produce illuminated addresses, and his daughter Mary excelled at working Celtic designs into these addresses. After landing the job of chief cartoonist for *The National Press*, he continued to draw the weekly supplement after the merger with *The Weekly Freeman* in 1892. Besides other commissions, "Fitz" also worked for *The Weekly Nation* and *The Irish Emerald*. In the 1890s he joined his former mentor, O'Hea, on *The Irish Figaro* (first called *The Dublin Figaro*), a breezy one-penny weekly edited by Sydney Brooks, one of Dublin's leading literary gadflies. In May 1905 Fitzpatrick realized his "cherished ambition" by launching his own humorous review, *The Lepracaun*, a monthly magazine of topical comment and satire which lasted until February 1915. "Fitz's" generosity won him many friends in Dublin—both rich and poor, but he was the kind of man who turned down the offer of a large subsidy from friends in order to have a completely free hand in running *The Lepracaun*. Until his health failed in 1911, he drew most of the black-and-white feature cartoons and illustrated advertisements in the review. Not being a weekly, *The Lepracaun* had time to think up sprightlier gossip and more pointed political comment. For these reasons as well as "Fitz's" warm personality and his dislike of Paddy jokes, *The Lepracaun* was one of Dublin's most readable reviews.[126]

Fitzpatrick's cartoons in this monthly often contained the ludicrous figure of John Bull with bulging eyes and paunch and heavy jowls—the epitome of a philistine.[127] Fitzpatrick also depicted the failings of John Redmond as a national leader, emphasizing his inability to prevent the youth of Ireland from joining the upstart party known as Sinn Fein. When Fitzpatrick fell ill in 1911, and his daughter Mary took over the editorship, O'Hea returned to draw some of the feature cartoons, among which "The Cat's-Paw" deserves mention, if only because John Bull appears here in the guise of a monkey

34 *"On the Ass's Back, Once More."* The Irish landlord stereotyped by an Irish nationalist. In this cartoon, John O'Hea tried to capture both the cruel, avaricious quality of his subject and the insolvency of this class. Note the tattered clothing and worn-out boot as well as the signs of summary injustice in his coat pocket. (From *The Weekly Freeman*, 4 December 1886.)

Irish Landlord.—"Ha! Ha! I'm on the Ass's back once more, and he will have to fall before he gets me off again. I know how to ride the brute, and I will make him carry me all over the country until every tenant is evicted who does not pay full rent, whether he has it or not—Oh! such a time we'll have."

using an Irish cat to snatch the burning coal of Irish trade from the fire.[128] Fitzpatrick also drew some first-class cartoons for *The Weekly Freeman and National Press*, including numerous variations on the landlord versus tenant theme. His figure of the insolvent and cruel Anglo-Irish landlord with thin face, drooping white moustache, monocle, and tattered clothes owed much to the stereotype favored by O'Hea in the 1880s, a good example of which may be seen in his cartoon for *The Weekly Freeman*, "On the Ass's Back, Once More" (4 December 1886). In "Tyrant and Toady" (17 September 1892), Fitzpatrick used almost the same figure with riding crop in hand in order to point out Pat's real enemies—the cadaverous landowner and the dandified Redmond, who refuses to use the party funds in Paris to relieve the evicted tenants. If the landlord resembles a choleric Anglo-Celt, Pat's features are cast in a more sanguine mold. The facial angles of Redmond and the landlord are roughly 76° and 72° respectively, but there are more pronounced differences between their physiognomies than a mere 4° would suggest.

35 *"Tyrant and Toady."* Images of the Irish made by an Irishman. Thomas Fitzpatrick reversed the English stereotyping process by making his hero, the evicted
tenant (second from the left) into an orthognathous and xanthous ideal type, being
advised by a somewhat more melanous but still handsome Pat of the National
Federation. The features of John Redmond and the rack-renting Irish landlord
speak for themselves. (From *The Weekly Freeman and National Press*, 17 September 1892.)

Redmond to the evicted tenants—"Go down on your knees to his Honour, and
perhaps he will take pity on you. If you don't you may starve. I will consent to
release the Paris Fund for his use, not yours."

Rackrenter—"No, no, friend John, I must make an example of the *base-born
peasant*. I thank your friends for teaching me that word."

Pat—"Cheer up, Comrade, I will stand by you to the last against false friend
or open foe. You have fought a brave battle, and the hour of victory is at hand."

Fitzpatrick could draw as prognathous a villain as the best English cartoonist when he wished to do so. A glance at the square-jawed, big-toothed
"Dynamitard" in his cartoon "Worthy Allies" should prove the point.[129] In
"Balfour's Bravos" a group of huge-mouthed, ferocious Ulstermen were
shown attacking Catholics in Belfast after being inflamed by Balfour's
speech at a Unionist demonstration there.[130] "Fitz's" finest monster, however, was a near replica of Matt Morgan's Fenian "Frankenstein" of 1870.
It is hard to believe that Fitzpatrick did not have a copy of *Tomahawk* close
at hand when he drew the figure of "Bigotry" in "The Frankenstein of
Hatfield and His Handiwork" (6 May 1893). This time Lord Salisbury was
cast as Dr. Frankenstein, and his monster's mission was to foment religious
riots in Belfast in order to undermine the Home Rule movement. In this

36 *"The Frankenstein of Hatfield and His Handiwork."* Thomas Fitzpatrick reversed Matt Morgan's "Irish Frankenstein" of 1869 by depicting the besotted figure of "Bigotry" being ordered by Lord Salisbury to return to his work of fomenting sectarian riots in Irish cities during the second Home Rule Bill debacle of 1893. (From color supplement of *The Weekly Freeman and National Press,* 6 May 1893.)

case, it took an Irish artist almost twenty years to reverse one of the more monstrous images created in London. The death of Fitzpatrick in February 1912 proved a major loss to the art of political cartoons in Ireland.

Another striking reversal of an English cartoon by an Irishman occurred in 1885 in a short-lived comic weekly called *The Irish Pilot or General Election Guide*. On 7 November there appeared a cartoon by an unsigned cartoonist called "The English Vampire" in which a horrifying vampire bat labeled "British Rule" was seen swooping down on beautiful Erin who was defending herself with a sword and a shield on which was written "National League."[131] This cartoon was a direct reply to Tenniel's "The Irish 'Vampire,'" which had appeared in *Punch* on 24 October. Tenniel had drawn a huge vampire with an evil face vaguely reminiscent of Parnell and symbolizing the National League, and this creature was about to attack the sleeping form of Erin. In this instance, it took only a fortnight for an Irish cartoonist to turn Tenniel's metaphor completely around.

Another cartoonist for *The Weekly Freeman and National Press* by the name of Phil Blake underlined the differences between English images and Irish realities in "The Contrast," which juxtaposed two scenes: one revealing a gentle Irish farmer peacefully protesting against land-grabbers who had taken an evicted holding; the other depicting a fiendish, drunken Englishman kicking his prostrate wife. The legend beneath this cartoon reads: "Criminal Ireland and Virtuous England; Which Needs Coercion?"[132] All the artists who drew for *The Weekly Freeman and National Press* adhered to the convention of honest, reliable Pat who was as angelic in his features as the Anglo-Saxonist image of Paddy was simian.

The London version of Paddy was also refuted by a young Irish cartoonist named Ernest Kavanagh (1884–1916), who was one of the "new" men of Dublin's labor movement. A good friend of Jim Larkin, "E.K." drew some penetrating cartoons in *Irish Freedom* and *The Worker* which attacked the exploitation of Dublin workingmen by the captains of industry and commerce. His mockery of the British recruiting drives in Ireland and his espousal of strike action in Dublin during 1913–14 won him thousands of working-class admirers. Kavanagh liked to bestow prognathous features on those who carried out the orders of Dublin Castle, and he gave these men huge mouths and bristling teeth which recall some of the Fenians drawn by London cartoonists in the 1860s. Kavanagh's promising career was cut short by British rifle fire which killed him on the steps of his beloved Liberty Hall soon after the outbreak of the Easter rebellion.[133]

Michael Reidy, principal artist of *Irish Fun* (1915–26) was one of the first Irishmen to use Celtic designs and lettering in his cartoons. Taking an ardent Sinn Fein line in politics, Reidy made mockery of Redmond's policies and carried the convention of handsome Pat well into the present century. This most Irish of Irish comic monthlies carried a serial story in Irish and kept shanty-Irish jokes to a strict minimum. A good example of both Reidy's technique and sympathies may be seen in "*This* Is Ireland's War" (January 1916), in which St. George, representing Irish industries, slays the hydra or dragon of foreign (i.e., British) manufactures, language, and rule—all of this drawn in a Celtic setting. Reidy's deadly serious tone presented a sharp contrast to the general run of parodies and jokes that filled the columns of *Irish Fun*.

Judging from the faces of Unionists and Loyalists that appear in Irish nationalist cartoons, one may conclude that Dublin's comic artists were neither as systematic nor as scientific in their treatment of the "enemy" as were their opposite numbers in London and New York. This is not to say that O'Hea, Fitzpatrick, and their fellow cartoonists were any less hostile to John Bull than were Tenniel, Proctor, and Morgan to Fenianism. But with a few notable exceptions, the nationalist cartoonists of Dublin preferred to make such enemies of Home Rule as policemen, Orangemen, and emergency men look brutal and prognathous rather than fully simian. Relatively few gorillas and orangutans inhabit Irish political cartoons between the 1860s and the 1920s. Most of Dublin's cartoonists preferred to turn their nationalist leaders into saints and martyrs or, at the very least, into fallen angels. Any nationalist unlucky enough to suffer the penalty of imprisonment, exile, or death for his devotion to the cause of independence was invariably canonized in the color supplements to the Home Rule newspapers.

No matter how provocative their intent, these nationalist cartoons were so many blunt banderillas that failed to puncture John Bull's tough old hide. Few Englishmen ever saw Dublin's weekly complement of political cartoons, and it is highly unlikely that these graphic protests against landlordism and English rule ever pricked the consciences of those ministers who decided Irish policy at Westminster. Dublin's cartoons were usually seen by men already converted to the cause, and it would be hard to prove that even the work of O'Hea brought in new recruits to the ranks of Home Rule. Occasionally, the response to a particular cartoon was loud and clear; but then the artist could not always be held responsible for the construction some viewers placed upon his work.

A case in point was the affair of the explosive cartoon. On the night of Saturday, 6 May 1893, a nitroglycerin bomb was hurled into the empty quadrangle of the Four Courts in Dublin. The explosion shattered scores of windows, but fortunately injured no one. Police and bomb experts rushed to the scene and found amidst the debris part of a canister and fuse. They also found a cartoon which had been extracted from the special Christmas number of *United Ireland* for 1889. This color supplement was unusual in that it had neither satirical nor comic content, but was a commemoration by two English artists of Gladstone's crusade for justice to Ireland. The art editor of *United Ireland* in 1889 had borrowed Henry Halliday's drawing of Hibernia and Britannia standing close together, while an angel hovered overhead holding a banner with the words "Peace on Earth—Goodwill

Towards Men." This etching had been commissioned for a mass meeting of the Liberal party held in St. James's Hall, London, on 3 March 1889. In the *United Ireland* version, this scene of sisterly love and imperial peace had been enclosed inside an elaborate border, drawn by Walter Crane, the gifted designer, book illustrator, and disciple of William Morris, in honor of Gladstone's golden wedding anniversary in July 1889. At the top of his neo-Gothic design, Crane had placed Gladstone in crusader's armor, holding a battle-axe labeled Home Rule. The grand old warrior was poised to slay a serpent whose many coils were marked with such evocative words as "Tyranny," "Coercion," "Eviction," and "Rack Rent." Caught in those ugly coils was a nameless maiden dressed in white. This pious composition was a far cry from the angry cartoons of J. D. Reigh in *United Ireland*. Because the explosion took place shortly after Gladstone's second Home Rule Bill had passed its second reading in the House of Commons and also eleven years to the day after the Phoenix Park murders, some newspapers suggested that the perpetrator was protesting against constitutional agitation and the Liberal formula known as "the Union of Hearts." If the so-called dynamiter had actually intended to draw attention to the Gladstone memorial cartoon, he must have been disappointed at the few lines given to its discovery and content in Dublin's papers. The *Irish Times* reporter did not mention the cartoon until several days after the blast and then gave a brief as well as inaccurate description of its message. Dublin's Home Rule press reminded readers that this was the fourth major explosion since 1891 and warned that such wanton acts could only jeopardize the cause.

In March 1894 the Irish nationalist writer and politician, Matthias McDonnell Bodkin, a member of Parliament, sent Gladstone a framed copy of this cartoon upon the announcement of Gladstone's intention to retire from politics. Bodkin explained that the bomb had been wrapped in a copy of this cartoon (without bothering to explain how it had survived the blast), and he added that "the real forces of disorder in Ireland are bitterly opposed to the policy of freedom for Ireland and friendship for the Empire which your genius has secured."[134] Had all of Dublin's cartoons been equally obnoxious to the dynamite and nitroglycerin wing of the republican movement, there might have been no public buildings left in Dublin for the men of Easter 1916 to occupy.

Dublin was not the only place to produce angelic Irish faces in popular periodicals. After the great famine, there were a few artists in London who made a special point of idealizing Irish features. These men were not really comic artists at all; they worked for the newer illustrated magazines or weeklies and were, in fact, the forerunners of the photojournalists of the late nineteenth century. There was no simianizing of Paddy in *The Illustrated London News*, founded in 1843, whose artists were paid to draw as much as possible from life rather than from fantasy. Before the camera began to dominate this topical weekly, the black-and-white illustrations tended to

37 *"Disturbed Ireland: Before the Magistrate."* Aloysius O'Kelly, the Irish-born illustrator, shows that simianized Calibans were not part of his equipment in this drawing of a young Irishman being tried for some offense connected with the land war. The artist's sympathies are clearly expressed in this attempt to convey the "realities" of the Irish question. (*Illustrated London News*, 5 February 1881.)

verge on the ideal and the sentimental, especially when and where human suffering was concerned. When the editors assigned several of their artists to cover the Irish land war in the early 1880s, the results provided a complete contrast to the cartoons of the comic weeklies. Instead of prognathous and simian brutes, the illustrations contained handsome, even noble faces which belonged to those tenants who dared to defend their cabins from evicting parties. Some of the most saint-like and orthognathous Celtic faces in this series were drawn by Aloysius C. O'Kelly, whose Irish origins may help to account for this effect. O'Kelly was born in Dublin in 1853 and aspired to become a serious artist, studying under Léon Joseph Florentin Bonnat (1883–1923) and Jean Léon Gérôme (1824–1904) in Paris. A number of his works were exhibited at the Royal Academy between 1876 and 1892. After spending several years on the staff of *The Illustrated London News*, O'Kelly emigrated to America where he settled in Brooklyn painting and teaching art.[135] An almost photographic memory combined with a profound sympathy for

38 *"The Irish Land League Agitation: Attack on a Process Server."* O'Kelly
again treats Irish faces in a more flattering manner in this drawing of an official
trying to serve notices of ejectment or eviction and being run out of town by the
aroused tenantry. (*Illustrated London News*, 21 May 1881.)

39 *"The Land League Agitation in Ireland: A Sheriff's Sale of Cattle, To Pay Rent."* In this illustration of a forced sale of cattle seized by the sheriff on a distraining order, O'Kelly endowed the crowd of onlookers—who presumably took no part in the bidding on orders from the Land League—with honest and orthognathous faces. (*Illustrated London News*, 18 June 1881.)

his countrymen heightened the dramatic effect of his drawings of Irish subjects, and such scenes as "Disturbed Ireland: Before the Magistrate," "The Irish Land League Agitation: Attack on a Process Server," and "The Land League Agitation in Ireland: A Sheriff's Sale of Cattle, To Pay Rent," show how easy it was for an artist who admired the Land League to ennoble the features of Irish tenants.[136] Another *Illustrated London News* artist who treated Irish physiognomies kindly was Richard Caton Woodville, an American who moved from Baltimore to London where he made his name as a painter of military panoramas. Besides his melodramatic rendering of "Disturbed Ireland: A Visit from 'Rory of the Hills'," Woodville also drew various other Irish scenes, including some which appeared in a Parisian weekly called *L'Univers Illustré*.[137] The French artists who helped to illustrate a special article on the Irish land question in 1880 also flattered the features of the men and women in the western counties of Ireland.[138] Not being cartoonists or caricaturists by profession, these men had no difficulty in awarding straight noses and high facial angles to Irish Celts, whether rural or urban, Home Rulers or loyalists.

Much the same treatment of Irish physiognomies could be found in *The Graphic* (1869–1923), which modeled itself on the same lines as *The Illustrated London News*. This topical London weekly sent artists to Ireland whenever royalty or that legendary leader of agrarian agitation, Captain Moonlight, visited the country, and the results were generally quite fair to Irish faces. Sydney Prior Hall, the son of Harry Hall the sporting artist of Newmarket, was assigned to cover the Queen's visit to Ireland in April 1885, and his illustrations of the crowds lining the Queen's route through town and country reveal very few signs of midfacial prognathism. There is one significant exception, however, and that is the face of the peasant in "Respectful Neutrality," a small sketch of a bystander who apparently refused to salute the Queen as she passed by, and kept his hands shoved into his pockets, according to the caption, lest he be tempted to wave.[139] The anonymous artists of *The Graphic* who illustrated the articles on Irish rural life in the 1870s and who covered the Phoenix Park murders in May 1882 made no attempt to Calibanize the "natives." On the contrary, they drew many pleasing Irish faces, even if most of these belonged to the female of the species.[140] In general, the artists who worked for London's topical magazines refrained from simianizing Paddy and avoided the cartoonists' favorite device of acute midfacial prognathism. If they indulged in any form of distortion, the results had more in common with angels or holy martyrs than with apes and monkeys.

Irish cartoonists and illustrators who worked in Dublin or farther afield, and who espoused Home Rule in some shape or form, thus sought to reverse the negative stereotypes used by those who preferred to simianize Paddy in the comic weeklies and monthlies of London and New York. Only a few examples of the response in Dublin to the simianization of Paddy have been cited here, but judging from the thousands of cartoons produced in Dublin during the Home Rule agitation, one may reasonably conclude that Irish cartoonists, and presumably those who saw their work, knew perfectly well what kind of image the comic weeklies of London were projecting. Many more pages would be required to convey the variety and individual flavor of Dublin's humorous periodicals in the later Victorian era. Far too little has been said about their literary or prose content, and nothing at all about the gradual introduction into these reviews of Irish language lessons and serialized stories in Irish garnished with Celtic motifs. But our primary concern has been the significance of apes and angels in cartoons, not the nature and function of comic periodicals and illustrated magazines in three metropolitan centers. Hopefully, the small sample adduced here will suffice to show that the simianized Paddy of Fleet Street and the Strand did not go

87

unchallenged in the British Isles. Handsome Pat, aided and abetted at times by beautiful Erin, was the champion chosen by Irish cartoonists to do battle with simianized Paddy or the Celtic Caliban of London and New York; and in Dublin, at least, there was no doubt as to which figure came closer to reality.

CHAPTER VII   # Fenian Physiognomies

UP TO THIS POINT we have looked at the images of Celtic Calibans, Irish Frankensteins, Irish vampires, and Irish apes produced by political cartoonists in London and New York, and we have seen some of the Irish angels drawn by Home Rule cartoonists in Dublin for home consumption. What about the reality or realities? Did some Fenians and Land Leaguers actually resemble the caricatures of Cruikshank, Tenniel, Proctor, Morgan, Bowcher, Furniss, and their equivalents in New York, or did they have more in common with the handsome, orthognathous Pats of O'Hea, Fitzpatrick, Reigh, and other cartoonists sympathetic to the cause of Irish nationalism? In the absence of reliable data about Irish facial features in the nineteenth century comparable with or equal to the morphological data collected by some physical anthropologists in the 1930s, we can only suggest that there was a grain of truth in both the prognathous and the angelic stereotypes of the Irish Celt. The accounts of Victorian tourists in Ireland, not all of them uninformed, the treatises of several reputable ethnologists, and a few photographs dating from the 1860s point to the existence of some midfacial prognathism and chin prominence as well as more regular features in the Irish population. But prognathism is not the same thing as simianism, Victorian caricature notwithstanding, and prominent chins do not a monkey make. The objective inquirer should ask not only how much prognathism in how many faces, but also, so what? Is there any demonstrable correlation of a positive sort between a long upper lip and a projecting mouth, on the one hand, and behavior on the other? The question may seem absurd, but many Victorians assumed axiomatically that there was such a correlation. Since the necessary data are lacking for the nineteenth century, it is not even possible to compare the facial angles of the populations of Great Britain and Ireland, not to mention those of Europe, Asia, Africa, and the Americas.

There are, however, enough clues scattered here and there in books, archives, and attics to permit a few generalizations about Irish faces in the nineteenth century, whether urban or rural, male or female, old or young. The best source for the student of Irish physiognomies is the photograph, and where they have not been too heavily touched up by a zealous portrait photographer, the impressions of the camera in Ireland may be usefully compared with the stereotypes of Paddy in Victorian comic weeklies and cartoons. Such a comparison reveals, not surprisingly, that those Irishmen who were lucky or unlucky enough—in the case of prison photographs—to have their faces recorded on film or glass for posterity had little in common with either apes or angels. The strikingly simian features of Tenniel's Irish dynamiters or Nast's Irish-American ward heelers bear even less relationship to reality than the saint-like faces of Pat the tenant farmer as drawn by O'Hea or O'Kelly. Evidence for this assertion may be found in various photographic collections in Dublin, among which are the photographs of roughly half of the six hundred or so men arrested after 1865 on suspicion of being Fenian activists. The files on these Fenian prisoners, which are now carefully preserved in the State Paper Office in Dublin Castle, contain, in addition to the slightly faded photograph, particulars about his identity, physical description, education, occupation, marital status, and activities. Many of these Fenian photographs were taken under adverse conditions: inadequate equipment and lighting no doubt tended to accentuate the less flattering lines and planes of the face which was bound to reflect the fatigue, strain, and overt hostility of the prisoner. Although many of these photographs are flawed, some might have been taken only a few years ago--so sharply delineated are the features. In the absence of better close-up pictures, these Fenian photographs provide a good idea of what some rank and file Fenians looked like as they were being booked, transferred, or released.

Less than half of the faces in these prison files reveal some marked degree of chin prominence—a feature of Irish morphology that conforms with the findings of E. A. Hooton and C. W. Dupertuis, the Harvard anthropologists who compiled that most important volume, *The Physical Anthropology of Ireland*. The five Fenian photographs reproduced here should convey some notion, however selective the sample, of the kinds of faces involved in the movement. There are faces in the Dublin Castle files which are uglier as well as more pleasing than these five.[141] Only about six of the three hundred or so photographs contain anything resembling acute midfacial prognathism, and it is not always easy to tell whether what used to be called the "potato mouth" owed more to the expression of the moment and dental neglect than to the configuration of the bones in the lower face. In any case, the ape-men and monsters of *Punch* and *Judy* are not to be found in this collection. And if one looks at the more prominent leaders of Fenianism, in particular John O'Leary, James Stephens, T. C. Luby, and the Irish-American John O'Mahony, one will find distinctly orthognathous and firm features beneath their intermittent beards.[142] In strictly morphological terms, there was little if anything to distinguish the Fenians from their captors—the members of the Royal Irish Constabulary who arrested them and the prison warders who guarded them.

In the rare photograph of "A Mass in the Mountains of Donegal," which was taken in 1867 by A. Ayton of Londonderry, when the camera was beginning to penetrate the Irish countryside, there are several fine examples of marked alveolar prognathism, chin prominence, and pronounced eyebrow ridges among the faces clearly visible in the first three or four rows.[143] Per-

*IRISH
REALITIES*

40–44 These Fenian prisoners were arrested in 1865–66 and in some cases their sentences ranged up to twenty years. (Photographs from the Fenian Papers in the State Paper Office, Dublin Castle.)

40 John Cade, age 22, was born in Drogheda, and served in the United States Army during the Civil War before returning to Ireland about 1865.

41 William Conn, age and address unknown, was released from Mountjoy jail in June 1884.

42 Timothy King, age 22, was an illiterate farmer from Millstreet, County Cork.

43 Mathew Regan, age 31, was a laborer born near Bally-mote, County Sligo, who worked for a time in England and then lived in Dublin where he was arrested.

44 J. Walshe. There is no description in his file.

haps these men were akin to those seen by John Beddoe and labeled thereafter "Africanoid." But before one jumps to the conclusion that these were Ireland's "Neanderthal and Cro-Magnon men," one should look more closely into the morphology of early man and one should ask too just how typical these "prognathous Celts" were of the population at large. There are more than two hundred and fifty persons worshipping at this outdoor chapel or

91

45　*A Mass in the Mountains of Donegal, 1867.* In this photograph of an Irish outdoor mass taken in 1867 at a scathlán in County Donegal, there are some striking examples of alveolar prognathism, chin prominence, and pronounced eyebrow ridges. But just how typical is this sample? (From *Sights and Scenes in Ireland*, page 173. Cassell and Co.: London, no date [1896].)

scathlán, and it would be the height of Victorian folly to assume that these features were to be found in every Donegal male, not to mention all Irishmen at home and abroad. The Victorian stereotype of the prognathous and huge-mouthed Irishman represented the wishful thinking of the viewer rather than the realities of Fenians, Land Leaguers, and Parnellites. Indeed, weak chests or tuberculosis were far more characteristic of Irish nationalists than acute midfacial prognathism; and, in any event, the real shape of the lower jaw was usually hidden from public view by a full beard which was shaved only after arrest and imprisonment or in order to make detection by the Special Branch more difficult.

Old notions and superstitions about the human face as a map of personality continue to hold their appeal, if only because they involve so little mental exertion and are far cheaper and quicker to come by than other forms of personality assessment. There are still educated men today who explain Irish prognathism in the nineteenth century as the result of diet (too many potatoes, and no meat) or of language (nature's reward for anyone foolish enough to master the complexities of Irish grammar and pronunciation). Another popular theory holds that environment shaped the features of the country people, as though the harsh poverty and climate of rural Ireland somehow molded the bones of the face. The burden of informed biological and anthropological opinion today, insofar as it can be understood by lay-men, points to genetic factors and the mechanisms of heredity as the determinants of man's morphological features. It is, therefore, to genes and chromosomes, not to diet or language, that one should look for the causes of upturned noses and prominent chins, wherever and whenever these are to be found among the races of man. However much the mental faculties of a child may be adversely affected by the dietary deficiencies of the mother during pregnancy, there is scant evidence to suggest that the child's jaw-bone or facial angle provides any indication of intelligence or character. It was the Victorian habit of equating degrees of prognathism with degrees of what seemed to be primitive behavior that endowed Paddy's facial angle with such political and social significance. The very concept of prognathism was a Victorian invention, with roots in the ancient lore of physiognomy, which fulfilled certain needs in the minds of the beholder or believer.

The serious student of Irish society past and present who seeks something more than impressions and hearsay about Irish facial features should consult the findings of the Harvard anthropological team that carried out a survey of over ten thousand Irish males in the 1930s. According to Hooton and Dupertuis, marked alveolar prognathism was *absent* in 97.7 percent of their sample of over eight thousand males. Midfacial prognathism was present in 8 percent and pronounced chin prominence was present in 9.3 percent of the same sample. Medium chin prominence was, however, discovered in 79.8 percent of those measured, and the findings of the investigators did reveal the existence of a "band of chin prominence all across the southern third of Ireland from Kerry to Wexford."[144] But the chins displayed in the photographs of subracial types in their appendix have nothing in common with the simianized brutes and beasts of Victorian caricature. Given the common tendency of men to ascribe to others those attributes they wish to deny in themselves, it may be pertinent to ask what kinds of jaws and chins the comic artists of London and New York were hiding beneath their beards. If that question appears too impertinent, then one can always turn to more obvious places for an explanation of the wide gulf between the images and the realities of Irish Fenians and Land Leaguers in the Victorian era.

93

CHAPTER VIII

The Cartoonists' Context

As Irishmen became more politically educated and turned to various kinds of political action in the nineteenth century ranging from republican and revolutionary to constitutional parties, and as tensions between landlords and tenants steadily mounted in the countryside, more and more Englishmen of property and respectability fell back upon the argument that Irish Celts, especially Roman Catholic Celts, could never be properly civilized or Anglicized. The Irish, in short, were a peculiar "race" with a temperament quite unsuited to English norms of rational behavior and political maturity. When applied to Irishmen, the word melancholy connoted not only an unfortunate concentration of black bile but an emotional instability which required firm Anglo-Saxon control in order to prevent serious trouble.

The exasperation of the Victorian governing classes with agrarian outrage and militant political agitation in Ireland found numerous outlets in English newspapers, pamphlets, history books, novels, and, of course, the comic weeklies. Schoolboys and undergraduates learned what little they knew about Irish Celtic character from Macaulay, Kingsley, Freeman, Froude, and Goldwin Smith, while their fathers and mothers read distorted articles about Ireland in *The Times* and perused the satirical pages of *Punch* or *Judy*. The stereotype of the primitive, melancholic, and prognathous Irish Celt was documented by anthropologists and ethnologists who constructed impressive typologies of the physiognomies of the British and Irish peoples. What remained of older physiognomical lore was absorbed into the newer sciences of craniology, anthropometry, and criminology, not to mention that favorite fad of freethinkers and radicals, phrenology. Those who professed these branches of the science of man added their weight to the popular belief that Celts were Celts, Saxons were Saxons, and that any mixture of the two races would debase the better blood and darken the fairer skin and hair. The heterogeneity or ethnic mixture of the inhabitants of the British Isles rarely deterred these men of science when it came to making categorical distinctions.

Although there were some men of letters and toleration in England who supported the grievances of Irish tenants, most middle- and upper-class Victorians preferred to see Paddy as a bundle of Celtic contradictions: a creature both happy and melancholy, drunk on whiskey and drunk on dreams, violent and gentle, lazy and capable of "working like a black," ignorant and cunning.[145] Because Paddy lacked self-control and emotional stability, it was easy for unscrupulous politicians to bring out the darker side of his melancholic temperament. The conviction of so many respectable people in England and Scotland that Irish temperament was determined by the blood or bile of the race served to reinforce the widespread objections to Home Rule that were based on religious and economic grounds. The efforts of Liberal and Radical Home Rulers to educate the British electorate about the justice of the Parnellite cause came too late and looked too expediential in 1886, with the Irish parliamentary party holding the balance between the two major parties, to change the dominant image of the wild Irish in most voters' minds. But the refusal of the Liberal party leaders and the new men of the Labour movement to believe that Irishmen were inherently unfit for self-government set an important example for their political heirs.

Some of the ingredients of the derogatory image of the Irish Celts were musty with age, but one does not have to go back to the time of Spenser, Moryson, and Davies to find descriptions of the Irish as a savage and barbarous people. John Pinkerton, the Scottish antiquarian and historian, wrote in his *History of Scotland*, published in 1797, that the Irish Celts were "savages, have been savages since the world began, and will be forever savages; mere radical savages, not yet advanced even to a state of barbarism."[146] During the campaign for Catholic Emancipation similar sentiments about the failings of the Irish found expression in the harangues of Protestant demagogues. Apart from profound religious differences, there were several good reasons why Irishmen were the object of overt prejudice in Great Britain. The existence of Fenianism and the Irish Republican Brotherhood, which in turn spawned even more secret and lethal societies, convinced many Victorians that the Irish preferred criminal and anarchist activities to constitutional politics. This conviction made it all the more difficult for Parnell in the 1880s to persuade the British electorate that his "new departure" did not represent the assassin, the arsonist, or the socialist. The quality of being Irish connoted varying degrees of inferiority to countless Victorians, all of whom chose to ignore the history of Anglo-Irish relations by blaming the absence of industry and industriousness in Ireland on the lack of enterprise in the Irish Celt.

Many members of the Victorian governing class believed that Irish inferiority was a more or less permanent state of affairs, the result of biological forces above and beyond the power of enlightened English administrators to control or ameliorate. Irish inferiority was seen as a function of Irish ethnicity, which in turn represented the conjunction of so-called Irish mental and physical traits as these had passed from one generation to the next in accordance with the laws of nature governing the transmission of hereditary characteristics. Irish Celts could no more change their temperaments than they could change the color of their eyes. This axiomatic belief in the continuity of Irish character for more than seven centuries was shared by many Englishmen who argued that the Irish Celts could not possibly manage their own affairs and therefore required English rule or what Sir Robert Peel once called "honèst, despotic government" to keep the "natives" in line. In physiognomical terms this meant that the melancholic and prognathous Celts had to be governed by sanguine, orthognathous men, otherwise the island would erupt into fratricide and anarchy. According to the Victorian version of the four humors, the Anglo-Irish garrison in Ireland was still considered sanguine enough to cope with the melancholic Celt, and the more choleric Anglo-Irish were expected to deal with the more phlegmatic peasantry. The trouble was that during the 1860s a familiar and dangerous hybrid was beginning to reappear—the unstable and ungovernable "melancholeric" rebel who represented the worst of two humors.

One striking feature of the simianized Irishman in cartoons was the heterogeneity of so many of those who were responsible for this stereotype. Few of London's leading cartoonists in this period belonged to what might be called the dominant ethnic group; and those most active in the simianizing of Paddy were frequently of Scottish rather than English extraction. The Lowlands in general and Edinburgh in particular proved a fertile breeding ground for various shades of Hibernophobia and anti-Celtic sentiment. Although born in London, James Gillray was the son of a Lanark man who had lost an arm at Fontenoy before settling in London. Similarly, George Cruikshank was the son of the Scottish illustrator and cartoonist, Isaac, who had emigrated to London in the 1780s. John Proctor came from Edinburgh, and Harry Furniss, who was born in Wexford, had a Scottish mother and a Derbyshire father.

Other cartoonists in the Victorian period were of mixed ancestry with a fair portion of what was called "Celtic blood" in their veins. John Leech's father was of Irish extraction. Tenniel's father, John Baptist, came from Huguenot stock, although he spent most of his life in Kensington. J. Kenny Meadows was born at Cardigan in South Wales, the son of a naval officer. Matt Morgan, presumably of Welsh origins, was born in London and died in New York. Some of the same exogenous patterns may be found among the cartoonists of New York City who flourished in the 1870s and 1880s. Nast was born in Landau, the son of a Bavarian bandmaster, and he came to America as a young child. Frank Leslie lured a number of British and European artists to New York to work for his *Illustrated Newspaper*, and from there they often moved on to draw for other weeklies. There was, in other words, a distinctly marginal quality about the condition of many cartoonists who apparently enjoyed making Irishmen and Irish-Americans look like apes. The absence of adequate biographical information about the bulk of these comic artists means that one can only speculate about the role of this marginality in shaping the kinds of stereotypes which these men conjured up in their cartoons.

To return to the Scottish Lowlands, there are other names, outside the ranks of cartoonists, which deserve mention in any survey of Hibernophobia. John Pinkerton was an Edinburgh antiquarian. The notorious anatomist and racist, Robert Knox, M.D., was an Edinburgh man who tried to earn a living by lecturing on the superiority of the Anglo-Saxon race after his dealings with the Irish body stealers and murderers, William Burke and William Hare, had ruined his medical career. Although in no way as hostile to Irish Celts as Knox, those two Scottish anthropologists, Daniel Mackintosh and Hector Maclean, produced none too flattering descriptions of Irish Celtic physiognomies in the 1860s and 1870s. And in the early 1890s an Edinburgh born and educated writer of Irish ancestry, Arthur Conan Doyle, created an arch villain of crime worthy of Sherlock Holmes's Anglo-Saxon mettle with the good Kerry name of Moriarty.[147]

It would be disingenuous to attempt to explain these attitudes towards Irish Celts simply in terms of Scottish nationalism, and it would be quite incorrect to dismiss them as irrelevant or extraneous because so many Scots supported Gladstone's Home Rule campaign during and after 1886. The fact is that there were few parts of the British Isles where anti-Irish prejudice had worked its way so deeply into the marrow of society than in the Scottish Lowlands. The widespread hostility toward the Irish in parts of Scotland derived much of its intensity from militant Protestants for whom denunciations of the Pope and all his so-called minions became a way of life. In addition to their Calvinistic or Knoxian resentment of anything that smacked of Rome, many Scottish Presbyterians despised the thousands of destitute and often diseased Irish immigrants who poured into the country during and after the great famine of the 1840s. Willing to take on any kind of menial labor for the lowest wages, these famine victims greatly increased the number of Irish-born already circulating in Scotland and equally desperate for regular employment. The steady flow of Irish laborers and their families into both rural and urban Scotland seriously aggravated religious, racial or ethnic, and economic tensions, and anti-Catholic sentiment became closely identified with anti-Irish feeling owing to the high correlation between Catholic and Irish in many areas. At the same time there were more than enough Irish Protestants in urban Scotland to trigger the fierce "Orange and Green" faction fights which earned many a headline in Scottish newspapers.[148]

During the 1850s popular Protestantism became even more rabble-rousing and violent in Scotland than in previous decades as fears about competition for jobs from cheap Irish labor and resentment about the rapid growth of Irish shantytowns fanned the flames of religious bigotry. Mass meetings, torchlight processions, crude demagoguery emanating from such preachers of "hate thy Catholic neighbor" as John Sayers Orr—the self-styled "Angel Gabriel," brutal attacks on Irish Catholic priests and laymen, the burning of Catholic chapels and Irish houses, and collusion between Protestant mobs and the local police proved that Scottish Protestants could be aggressive as

well as bigoted, if any proof was needed. A typical piece of anti-Irish reporting in *The Scottish Guardian* described a woman from Connaught as having
"the unmistakable width of mouth, immense expanse of chin and 'forehead
villainous low' so characteristic of the lowest Irish." The writer then drew
attention to "the proverbially belligerent disposition of the half-civilized,
and wholly Romanised savages."[149] Selections from another staunch Protestant paper, *The North British Daily Mail*, show how fond some journalists
were of degrading Irish features: "an ape-faced, smallheaded Irishman";
"Pat O'Shannon, a startled-looking Irish tailor, with a cruel Tipperary
visage"; and "Michael McLaughlin, a blackguard-looking creature with a
plastered face."[150]

The activities of Fenians in Ireland after 1865 sparked a revival of violent
anti-Irish feeling, especially in the Glasgow and Greenock area, and the
amount of panic-mongering in the press about the hordes of armed Fenians
drilling and looting at night in the Scottish countryside revealed the profoundly irrational nature of popular Protestantism. Even before the bloody
Clerkenwell explosion in December 1867, *The Glasgow Herald* was busy
inflaming Protestant prejudices with articles on the Fenian menace, including one special report entitled "A night among the Fenians, and other wild
animals."[151] Given the widespread animus of so many Protestant Scots
against the Catholic Irish, it is less difficult to account for the Scottish contribution to the derogatory image of the Irish Celt in Victorian cartoons. And
given, too, the fact that many Lowlanders knew that Englishmen and Irishmen tended to regard them as half-breeds or ethnic hybrids—in some cases
the term "mongrel dog" was used by those who regarded themselves as
purer Celts—it is just possible that some Lowlanders found a natural scape-
goat for their own hybridity in an ethnocentric age in the form of the
Irish-Catholic Celt. No doubt there are several other equally plausible
explanations of the psychology of simianization by cartoonists in the Victorian era, but so little is known about the inner thoughts of these comic
artists and illustrators that the latent content of their work continues to elude
precise definition. It is possible, nevertheless, to conclude that Scottish
artists and scientists as well as pseudoscientists played a far more decisive
part in shaping English images of the Irish in the nineteenth century than
has hitherto been realized.

Lastly, there is the evolutionary significance of the simianized Irish Celt
in Victorian caricature. Both the content and the timing of this stereotype
suggest that much of the cartoonists' inspiration derived from the great
controversy of the 1860s about the origins of human and animal life and the
mechanisms of evolution. The desire of men to attribute animal features and
instincts to their fellow men, while reserving either human or divine attributes to themselves, must be as old as man's first awareness of the differences
in behavior between himself and the higher forms of vertebrate life. Monkeys and men have been the objects of analogous, homologous, and humor-

ous observations since ancient times, and long before the lectures and treatises of Victorian naturalists on the resemblances between man and the Simiidae, comparisons and metaphors were being made in which men and monkeys were closely associated. As Horst W. Janson's fascinating book attests, the simian form was often used during the Renaissance and Reformation in art and literature to represent everything from lust to laughter and mimicry to deviltry.[152] The process of simianizing the stereotypical Irishman, on the other hand, belongs in all essentials to the middle decades of the nineteenth century.

What was relatively new about the simian image of Paddy was not the sense conveyed thereby of Celtic inferiority and Anglo-Saxon superiority, which was a subjective state of affairs with a long history, but rather the scientific impulse behind that image. Admittedly the simianization of Paddy began before the publication of Charles Darwin's *The Origin of Species*, but so too did the debate among natural scientists about the ancestry of man and his relationship to the quadrumana. The full-blown image of the ape-like Irishman began to appear in cartoon and caricature in the early 1860s at just about the same time as information about the great apes—in particular the gorilla and the orangutan, with which the former was often confused —was disseminated in newspapers, popular magazines, and scientific journals. For most Victorians of this era the gorilla was a new discovery, having been positively identified in Africa only in the later 1840s. One may presume that few Victorians had read Dr. Thomas S. Savage's article on gorillas in the *Boston Journal of Natural History* published in 1847, but countless visitors to the British Museum may have seen their first stuffed gorilla in a glass case in the Natural History Collection there. The word itself derives from *gorillae* or "the wild men" seen by Hanno of Carthage in his voyage south of the Pillars of Hercules. It is worth noting that the word gorilla does not appear in the eighth edition of the *Encyclopaedia Britannica*, published in Edinburgh in 1856–57, wherein the apes are subsumed under the general section of "Mammalia."[153] The ninth edition of the *Britannica*, published in 1875, atoned for this neglect by devoting an entire article to "Apes" in which the author, St. George Mivart, the zoologist, placed *"Troglodytes gorilla"* of West Africa alongside *"Troglodytes niger"* (the chimpanzee) as the two mammals closest to man in all physiological respects.[154] The myth of a race of ape-men or "missing links" living in the depths of central Africa was given a new lease of life in Victorian imaginations by the arrival of a live gorilla at the London Zoological Gardens in 1860. The first adult gorilla to land in England, this creature attracted throngs of visitors. The publicity given to the anthropoid apes in the early 1860s had much to do with the famous controversy between the defenders of the faith and the champions of Darwin over the origins of human and animal life. For the first time it was possible for Victorians to observe the behavior of their closest relative in the animal world now behind bars at the London Zoo.

In the comic weeklies of the 1860s jokes about apes and their resemblance to man became the fashion. The first number of *Fun* (21 September 1861) contained Brennan's cartoon of "The Gorilla Family at the Sea-Side" in which father and mother gorilla and their relations were dressed like eminently respectable Victorians on holiday at a seaside resort, while a few startled human beings looked on.[155] A month later one of *Fun's* artists drew a picture of Thomas Huxley arm in arm with a gorilla on a lecture platform.[156] Then, on 11 January 1862, *Fun* carried a small drawing of a semi-simian Irish politician, The O'Donoghue, member of Parliament for Tipperary, which was entitled "The Irish Blackguard." Next to him was the even more ape-like face of his wife.[157] Presumably this was *Fun's* way of celebrating the outspoken remarks of Daniel O'Connell's nephew in the House of Commons. As if to drive the point home, one of *Fun's* writers pondered the return of several stuffed gorillas to the office window of *The Field* and suggested (8 March 1862) that they might have been away in Ireland visiting their relative, The O'Donoghue.[158]

The link between anthropoid apes and Irish Celts was made quite explicit by an unknown writer in *Punch* in the same year (18 October 1862), who concocted the following delightful fantasy under the title, "The Missing Link":

> A gulf, certainly, does appear to yawn between the Gorilla and the Negro. The woods and wilds of Africa do not exhibit an example of any intermediate animal. But in this, as in many other cases, philosophers go vainly searching abroad for that which they would readily find if they sought for it at home. A creature manifestly between the Gorilla and the Negro is to be met with in some of the lowest districts of London and Liverpool by adventurous explorers. It comes from Ireland, whence it has contrived to migrate; it belongs in fact to a tribe of Irish savages: the lowest species of the Irish Yahoo. When conversing with its kind it talks a sort of gibberish. It is, moreover, a climbing animal, and may sometimes be seen ascending a ladder laden with a hod of bricks.
>
> The Irish Yahoo generally confines itself within the limits of its own colony, except when it goes out of them to get its living. Sometimes, however, it sallies forth in states of excitement, and attacks civilised human beings that have provoked its fury.
>
> The somewhat superior ability of the Irish Yahoo to utter articulate sounds, may suffice to prove that it is a development, and not, as some imagine, a degeneration of the Gorilla.[159]

It would be easy to dismiss this gibe as a piece of light-handed frivolity were it not for the manner in which London's leading cartoonists depicted the Irish Frankenstein and Caliban during and after the Fenian era. Other examples of the popular association between Pongidae and Irishmen include John Leech's portrayal of John Mitchel as a monkey in *Punch* in 1848 and Charles Kingley's description of the poor peasants he saw in County Mayo and Connemara in 1860 as "white chimpanzees."[160] Later in the century, a new chimpanzee was brought to the London Zoo to replace the late and much lamented "Sally." The new inmate was called "Paddy," and an amusing article in *The Strand Magazine* described him as follows: "For Paddy is certainly a gentleman, since he wipes his mouth after drinking, and would be a master of polite manners could he overcome his shyness."[161]

All caricature is by definition a distortion of reality, and it would be absurd as well as futile to take caricaturists or cartoonists to task because they chose to exaggerate or invent a particular set of physical features in order to make their points. The question that concerns us here is not the right of comic artists to turn Irishmen into apes or monkeys, but rather why so many cartoonists on both sides of the Atlantic preferred the simian rather than the porcine, canine, asinine, feline, bovine, or lupine metaphor for Paddy. Every so often one encounters a pig-headed or potato-faced Irishman in London's comic weeklies, but these are few and far between compared with the ape-men. After the midcentury, Paddy was rarely drawn as a leprechaun or as a rollicking, drink-sodden stage Irishman except by artists in Dublin. If there were, in fact, far more Irishmen who appeared to conform to English notions of the stage Irishman than there were Fenians, it is worth asking why Paddy became so simian in the 1860s and after. Irishmen were often considered savage and barbarous by learned men in England and Scotland during the eighteenth century, and we have Pinkerton's testimony that "what a lion is to an ass, a Goth is to a Celt." Even so the stereotypical Irishman of the late eighteenth and early nineteenth century, however nasty and brutish his lower jaw, remained patently human rather than bestial. During the 1860s, however, Paddy became a simianized Caliban who seemed to belong behind bars. In a biological sense, Paddy had devolved, not evolved, from a primitive peasant to an unruly Caliban, thence to a "white Negro," and finally he arrived at the lowest conceivable level of the gorilla and the orangutan. This impression of the physical degeneration taking place in Ireland reflected a marked change in Victorian attitudes about the place of the races of man in the hierarchy of nature rather than any serious increase in the rebelliousness of the Irish people.

Paddy won his simian features not just because of his propensity to resort to dynamite and firearms in order to end British rule in his country; after all, Irishmen had been plotting rebellions for centuries. The timing of his transmogrification into a gorilla suggests that the coincidence of Fenianism with the debate over *The Origin of Species* and the increase in social and political tensions arising out of the economic expansion of the mid-Victorian era lay at the root of the simianizing process. The pressures of upward social mobility were already disturbing the recently entrenched middle classes who had no wish to share their status and neighborhood with even skilled laborers and other members of the working-class elite. Fenianism, with its active branches in the midst of urban England and Scotland, conjured up in many middle- and upper-middle-class minds such specters as mob rule,

Romanism, republicanism, anti-imperialism, and the desire of the "lower orders" to demolish the existing social system. Respectable Victorians, anxious to preserve the status quo which favored them, tended to regard Fenianism as an Irish manifestation of the growing challenge to constituted authority at home. Just as Darwinism appeared to lay bare the ugly realities of the struggle for survival, so Fenianism appeared to reveal the elemental beast in Irish character. Since the Fenians were treated in British newspapers as little better than thugs bent on murder and dealing in treason without any legitimate grievances to speak of, they were categorized as dangerous political criminals; and the criminal classes, especially those involved in crimes of violence against persons, were already being depicted in cartoons and book illustrations as acutely prognathous brutes with enormous jaws and tiny brains.[162]

The glaring publicity given to Fenian attacks and dynamitings in the English and Scottish press fanned the widespread prejudice against the Catholic Celtic Irish, and many Victorians began to believe that if there were any "missing links" in the British Isles, they were to be found in Ireland. What did the word anthropoid really mean to educated Victorians? There was a disturbing ambiguity about a term that could be stretched to include either a man-like ape or an ape-like man. The same kind of ambiguity applied to such words as troglodyte, satyr, and gorilla. To confuse the issue further, many Victorians failed to distinguish between monkeys and apes. Carlo Pellegrini (1839–89), the Italian artist and bon vivant, who made his fortune in London as the peerless creator of *Vanity Fair's* cartoons of eminent Victorians, signed his first contribution, a drawing of Disraeli in 1869, with the pen name "Singe." Shortly thereafter he adopted the new signature with which he became famous, namely "Ape."[163] In the context of the 1860s this change was not without significance. In addition, the great apes were widely held to be aggressive and vicious creatures, quite capable of attacking men as well as carrying off young maidens into the jungle for carnal purposes. Ironically enough, Daniel O'Connell, whose philandering was the talk of more than County Kerry, was once accused by a political opponent of being as "capricious as the ouran outang in your amours."[164] Given the reputation of the quadrumana for sexual activity of every kind, it required no great ingenuity for Victorians to assign simian features to the wild Irish Celt. In the presence of so much conflicting evidence about the alleged sexual prowess or reticence of Irish males in the nineteenth century, one can only speculate about the libidinous content of the simian idiom in English cartoons.

In seeking an explanation for the simianizing of Paddy, it is not necessary to inflate the reputation of *The Origin of Species* as a traumatic event in the lives of those Victorians who bothered to venture beyond the title page. Long before the publication of Darwin's treatise, suspicions were growing about the threat of natural science to both the sanctity of scripture and the nobility of man. The decades leading up to 1859 were crowded with hypotheses about the origins of life, the antiquity of the earth, and the varieties of the human and animal species.[165] In the late 1850s Thomas Huxley was preparing a series of lectures for popular consumption on the relation of man to the animals, with special emphasis on the quadrumana, and it was this explosive topic that captured the limelight at the famous meeting of the British Association in Oxford in 1860. According to Huxley, the gradual erosion of the traditional barriers separating homo sapiens from the man-like apes had touched off a "running fight" between evolutionists in the mold of Sir Richard Owen the anatomist, and traditionalists, whose champion was Samuel Wilberforce, the bellicose bishop of Oxford. What *Punch* called "the gorilla controversy" had much to do with Huxley's inquiry into the resemblances between man and the anthropoid apes and monkeys. Regarding the place of man in the hierarchy of nature as "the question of questions," Huxley tried to convince his audiences that the primate which came closest to man "in the totality of its organisation" was either the chimpanzee or the gorilla.[166] With considerably more tact, Charles Darwin also discussed the kinship of the anthropoids in his *Descent of Man*, published in 1871, which contained many homologous observations about human and animal physiology and behavior. Darwin's remark that man was, in fact, an "off-shoot from the Old World Simian stem" was hardly likely to allay the anxieties of readers who had been brought up to believe in the divine origins of mankind.[167] One wonders just how many God-fearing as well as vain Victorians resented having their brains and bodies compared to "*Pithecus satyrus, Troglodytes niger*," or "*Gorilla gorilla*." It would have been most natural for these traditionalists to make their own comparisons and to find resemblances between the anthropoid apes and those whom they feared or despised— namely Irish dynamiters, African savages, or their own criminal classes. Fearing Darwinism as a threat to both their own dignity and the authenticity of Genesis, these Victorians found some comfort in Wilberforce's sardonic reference to simian ancestry which Huxley had countered so artfully at Oxford in 1860.

However fragmentary and tenuous the evidence may be, there are clues in both Victorian literature and caricature which indicate that those who were most disturbed by the prospect of being cousin to apes and monkeys derived some temporary relief by treating the Irish and other lesser breeds around the world as a buffer or evolutionary cordon sanitaire between themselves and the anthropoid apes. If there was any substance at all to the theory that gorillas were man's nearest relatives in the animal world, then it was quite possible to argue that some races of man were closer to them than others. It was comforting for some Englishmen to believe—on the basis of the best scientific authority in the Anthropological Society of London— that their own facial angles and orthognathous features were as far removed from those of apes, Irishmen, and Negroes as was humanly possible.

Among the established and propertied classes in England such relatively new expressions as natural selection, the struggle for existence, and Spencer's famous phrase "the survival of the fittest" meant something less impersonal or abstract than competition in a state of nature. Perceptive Victorians recognized in these terms the dynamics of class struggle. So too did the Marxists. Social Darwinism was the ideological result—some would call it a perversion—of applying the so-called law of the jungle or the mechanisms of natural selection to man, or rather to men grouped together in families, classes, nations, empires, and races. The Fenians seemed to be so "red in tooth and claw" because they were allegedly inspired by class hatred and were prepared to kill or be killed. English journalists and cartoonists helped to feed the growing popular hysteria after 1865 by depicting the Fenians and their successors in the Land League and other Irish revolutionary societies as criminal ape-men (or was it ape-like criminals?) who deserved to be hanged or imprisoned behind bars for life like the monkeys and apes at the zoo.

The simianizing of Paddy in the 1860s thus emanated from the convergence of deep, powerful emotions about the nature of man, the security of property, and the preservation of privilege. Since the very integrity of English civilization seemed to be menaced by Darwinism, democracy, republicanism, socialism, and Fenianism, one convenient way of epitomizing those fears was to shift the burden of proximity to the gorillas onto the burly shoulders of those Irish agitators who wanted nothing better than to strike terror into the hearts of their oppressors. In Ireland, by contrast, the forces of democracy and Darwinism had barely made headway against the strong resistance of a traditional society. Upward social mobility was visible only in the more advanced urban centers of Belfast and Dublin, and even there the vertical division between Roman Catholic and Protestant affected the whole social structure. The publication of *The Origin of Species* seems to have caused only a few ripples in Ireland, and most of those barely reached the outer perimeter of the Anglo-Irish pale. The stark contrast between political arrangements, social structure, and religion in England and Ireland during the nineteenth century may help to account for the relative scarcity of simianized Anglo-Saxons in Irish cartoons and comic weeklies. Not that the faces of John Bull, Orangemen, and Anglo-Irish landlords drawn in Dublin inspired trust or admiration. Dublin's political cartoonists, as we have already seen, made the lackeys of Dublin Castle, especially police constables and emergency men, look decidedly prognathous and brutish. But they were not in the habit of using the simian device as regularly as the leading cartoonists of London and New York. Irishmen, one should add, found ample opportunity for expressing their feelings about English rule in speech and writing; and the violent language of even moderate Home Rulers after the advent of Parnell reveals much about the quality of Irish nationalism.

The gorilla metaphor cropped up often after the outbreak of rebellion in 1916, followed by the Anglo-Irish guerrilla war of 1919–21. Combatants and their intended victims naturally saw one another as brutal and bestial, and the reprisals that took place before the cease-fire in 1921 had the effect of lowering the facial angles of the enemy, whoever he might be. A striking example of the simian image in this era of "the troubles" comes from the autobiography of Sir Christopher Lynch-Robinson, who, like so many of his caste, thought of himself as a good Irishman, no matter how Unionist his politics, Protestant his faith, and Ascendancy his forebears. Although a loyal servant of the Crown, remaining as Resident Magistrate for County Louth until the bitter end, Lynch-Robinson was horrified by the Black and Tan recruits sent over by the British authorities to bolster the ranks of the Royal Irish Constabulary. One day he walked into the police barracks at Drogheda, where he was well-known, and found himself facing one of the new Black and Tan recruits. In his own words:

> He was an ape-like creature, sprawling all over the table at which he was sitting. His uniform was unbuttoned, he had long, wet hair hanging down over his eyes, and there was a smell of whisky off him that would intoxicate a wasp. On seeing me, he reached for a revolver lying on the table in front of him, pulled the hammer back with his thumb, and pointing it unsteadily at me, mumbled: "Who the —— hell are you?" The Black and Tans were new to me at that time, and I hadn't the foggiest idea what this baboon was, sitting there in police uniform, drunk to the world at eleven o'clock in the morning.[168]

Fortunately for the Resident Magistrate, the regular Royal Irish constable on duty intervened just in time to prevent him from being shot as a Sinn Feiner by the recruit. Shortly after this harrowing incident, Lynch-Robinson was attending court at Trim in County Meath, and he noticed that a group of Black and Tans had been assigned to guard the courthouse and protect him.

> I nearly jumped out of my skin at the mere sight of them. They were like a bunch of gorillas. They had india-rubber looking faces, large ears, big fat lips, and most of them had that blank, uncanny expression of the *crétin*. The officer and the two sergeants in charge were obviously afraid of them, and I felt the whole time as if I were amongst homicidal maniacs that might run amuck at any moment.[169]

Lynch-Robinson was no Sinn Feiner, and he had no time for gun-slinging republicans. Isolated though he was from "the main stem of the Irish nation," he loved Ireland and knew the country almost as well as his father, Sir Henry Robinson, who for years was the head of the Irish Local Government Board. In view of Sir Christopher's credentials, one may well wonder if there was not some basis in fact for his description of these twentieth-century, paramilitary, English adventurers.

The images of the Irish Celt in Victorian times thus depended on the

DRESSING FOR AN OXFORD BAL MASQUÉ.

"THE QUESTION IS, IS MAN AN APE OR AN ANGEL? (*A Laugh.*) NOW, I AM ON THE SIDE OF THE
ANGELS. (*Cheers.*)"—Mr. Disraeli's *Oxford Speech, Friday, November 25.*

46 "*Dressing for an Oxford Bal Masqué.*" Tenniel's sublime cartoon of Disraeli
admiring his angelic features in the mirror captures both the comedy and the
anxiety of those Victorians who saw in the evolutionary theories of Darwin and
Huxley nothing more than a choice between ancestral apes and angels. (*Punch,*
10 December 1864.)

perspective of the viewer and the features he was determined to find or to exaggerate. Englishmen who celebrated the genius of the Anglo-Saxon race tended to see themselves as modern Athenians, endowed with Grecian noses and facial angles in the high eighties or low nineties. These men thought that the common Catholic Irishman was the antithesis of all these desirable qualities: Paddy was a wild, melancholic, indolent, unstable, and prognathous Caliban with a facial angle in the low sixties. After the outbreak of Fenian violence in the mid-1860s, Paddy descended further to find himself a niche somewhere between the "white Negro" and the anthropoid apes. Other Victorians, slightly more tolerant in outlook, saw some virtue here and there in Irish character in spite of the corrosive effects of Irish history and drink, and they assumed that the Irish people could still be effectively ruled from Westminster provided that the law was applied in a firm and consistent manner. A small minority of Victorians, on the other hand, genuinely sympathized with Irish grievances and the Home Rule movement, and these less prejudiced men believed that on the whole Irishmen were no lazier, darker, drunker, or more prognathous than their own countrymen.

If Victorians really did have a choice between apes and angels as their ancestors, then most of them preferred to follow Disraeli's example, so brilliantly satirized by Tenniel in "Dressing for an Oxford Bal Masqué,"[170] by opting for the angels. It was only meet and right for respectable, not to say narcissistic, Victorians to insist that they were descended from the heavens rather than the trees. But preference for a paradise lost was one thing: certitude about either the origins of man or the physical and mental differences between some men and the great apes in an age of increasing deference to natural science was another matter. By the 1870s an enlightened Victorian might well wonder just how different in physiology an English gentleman, for all his classical education and civilization, was from the untutored, primitive Irish peasant, and the gorilla. The homologous studies of the Darwin–Wallace–Huxley school could not be dismissed so glibly as Bishop Wilberforce and his disciples liked to believe. Growing ever more uneasy about the apparent contradictions of the Bible by natural scientists, especially after the publication of Darwin's *The Descent of Man*, orthodox scripturalists had to indulge in some hasty rationalizing in order to deny their own proximity to the animal kingdom and, by extension, to deny the homologous beast within themselves. Anxious to stay as close as possible to the angels, some of these worthy Christians found reassurance in the thought that the nearest relatives of the anthropoid apes among mankind lived in out of the way places such as Africa, Asia, India, and even Ireland, where they could be observed as well as controlled without too much danger of contamination. Because Irish Celts seemed increasingly unwilling or unable to conform to Anglo-Saxon standards of self-control and civility, they began to look ever more simian to those who resented the Irish for being Irish. Anglo-Saxons, after all, could never be accused of having the same physiognomies as Irish Celts. Was it not Pope Gregory I who had observed, when passing by a group of fair-haired British youths on sale in the Roman slave market: "Non Angli, sed Angeli?"[171]

The trouble with some Victorians, especially after 1859, was that while they wanted to be both, they feared, deep down, that they might be neither.

Notes

[1] Molinari spent some years in Paris as a young man writing for the more advanced radical newspapers before returning to his native Brussels in 1851 to take up the chair of political economy at the Museum of Industry. His letters to the *Journal des Débats* on the condition of Ireland were later published under the title, *L'Irlande, le Canada, Jersey*. Molinari's phrase "une variété de negres blancs" appeared in translation in a leader in *The Times* of London on 18 September 1880.

[2] For a brief and allusive treatment of these comparisons, see L. P. Curtis Jr., *Anglo-Saxons and Celts*, pages 49-65. Field Marshal Wolseley once referred to the Sudanese "murderers" of his good friend Colonel Stewart in 1884, while on the Nilotic expedition, as "cowardly skulking reptile[s] such as this country and Ireland produces in large numbers." Quoted in Adrian Preston, editor, *In Relief of Gordon*, page 57.

[3] There is no modern, let alone definitive, history of physiognomy from Hippocrates to the present, but a useful introduction to this subject may be found in the *Encyclopaedia Britannica*, 11th edition, volume 21, pages 550-52, in an article by Professor Alexander Macalister of the Faculty of Anatomy at Cambridge University. One of the classic texts on physiognomy in the pre-Lavaterian era was produced by the Neapolitan savant, Giovanni Battista Della Porta, entitled *De Humana Physiognomonia*, which passed through numerous editions in the seventeenth century.

[4] Second edition, page 6.

[5] Ibid., pages 57-58.

[6] *Hard Times* (New York: W. W. Norton and Company, Inc., 1966), page 1.

[7] Modern Library edition, 1946, page 596.

[8] Pages 12-13.

[9] Ibid., pages 125-26.

[10] The original version of the nature of the four moist humors may be found in Hippocrates, *Works*, translated by W. H. S. Jones, pages 2-41, 62-95. A brief discussion of classical physiology appears in Charles Singer, *A Short History of Anatomy and Physiology from the Greeks to Harvey*, pages 9-36. Classical humoralism was given a new lease on life in this century when the neurophysiologist, Pavlov, divided his dogs in the laboratory into the four humoral categories or temperaments of the Hippocratic school in order to classify and explain their reactions to stress and various stimuli. This same classification was also applied to the victims of shell shock and combat fatigue by some doctors in British hospitals during World War II. See William Sargant, *The Battle for the Mind*, pages 29-63.

[11] Aristotle's writings on the physiognomy of animals and man may be found in *The History of Animals of Aristotle and His Treatise on Physiognomy*, translated by Thomas Taylor, pages 421-46.

[12] One of the most popular versions of Lavater's work was the translation by Thomas Holcroft, *Essays on Physiognomy* (fifth edition, 1848). This edition also contained the following useful account, "The Memoirs of the Life of the Author Compiled Principally from The Life of Lavater, by G. Gessner." The eighteenth edition of this work was published in 1885.

[13] For Camper's anatomical and physiognomical theories, see T. Cogan, editor, *The Works of the Late Professor Camper on the Connection between the Science of Anatomy and the Arts of Drawing, Painting, Statuary*. The illustrations of Camper's facial angle, reproduced here as Figure 1: 1-4 and Figure 2: 1-4, are taken from Tables I and II which were published in 1794 and bound into this edition.

[14] Camper explained his methods of obtaining the facial angle and other skull measurements in Part 1, chapters 3-4, of this work. He arranged his small collection of skulls on a shelf in his study in the following order: "apes, orangs, negroes, the skull of an Hottentot, Madagascar, Celebese, Chinese, Moguller, Calmuck, and divers Europeans." Ibid., page 50.

[15] Blumenbach criticized Camper's angle because it did not take into account any lateral

extension of the face, and because Camper lacked an adequate sample of skulls that might have shown how much variation existed in facial lines or angles within the same national or racial unit. He also accused Camper of inconsistency in applying his criteria of measurement to the skulls in his possession. See *The Anthropological Treatises of Johann Friedrich Blumenbach*, translated and edited by Thomas Bendyshe, pages 121–24. Further strictures on the facial angle may be found in *An Essay on the Causes of the Variety of Complexion and Figure in the Human Species By Samuel Stanhope Smith*, edited by Winthrop D. Jordan, pages 178–181.

[16] The standard English translation of Blumenbach's classic work was produced by Thomas Bendyshe under the auspices of the Anthropological Society of London in 1865. This edition contains extracts from his dissertation, *De Generis Humani Varietate*, first published in 1775, as well as from his *Contributions to Natural History* (1790).

[17] Bell also cast some doubt on Camper's theories about the connection between national character, facial beauty, and facial angle. For his discussion of skulls and head forms, see the second essay, pages 23–48. The drawings of "rage" and "madness" on pages 139 and 153 respectively bear some resemblance to Erskine Nicol's striking portrait of a wild Irishman, called "Home Rule," reproduced in Mrs. S. C. Hall's *Tales of Irish Life and Character* (London, 1909), facing page 24.

[18] Darwin denied any concern with physiognomy, which he defined as "the recognition of character through the study of the permanent form of the features," page 1. For his praise of Bell, see pages 2–3, 9, 49–50. One wonders if the alleged objections of Captain Fitz-Roy of the *Beagle* to the size and shape of Darwin's nose in 1831 may not have soured the scientist on Lavaterian physiognomy for the rest of his life.

[19] Prichard, *Researches into the Physical History of Man*. For his monogenist convictions, see especially the preface and chapters 1–3.

[20] Ibid., pages 165–73. For Prichard's views on Celtic physiognomy and ethnology, see ibid., pages 526–35, and also *The Eastern Origin of the Celtic Nations*. There is a helpful discussion of Prichard's contributions to the treatment of mental illness in England in Denis Leigh, *The Historical Development of British Psychiatry*, volume 1, pages 148–209.

[21] Traces of classical humoralism may be seen in John Beddoe's work, *The Races of Britain, A Contribution to the Anthropology of Western Europe*. Beddoe derived many of his working assumptions from such physical anthropologists and craniologists as Paul Broca, Rudolf Virchow, and J. Barnard Davis.

[22] Relatively little of the work of Anders Adolf Retzius (1796–1860) was translated into English during his lifetime, but an exception was his "Present State of Ethnology in Relation to the Form of the Human Skull" in *Annual Report of the Smithsonian Institution, 1859*, pages 251–70.

[23] Anyone interested in phrenology should consult not only Alexander Macalister's article in the *Encyclopaedia Britannica*, 11th edition, pages 534–41, but John D. Davies's study of the American varieties, *Phrenology, Fad and Science*. Besides London and New York, Edinburgh provided a most sympathetic climate for this cult. The *Phrenological Journal and Miscellany* published there was continued from 1838 to 1847 as *The Phrenological Journal and Magazine of Moral Science*, new series, in ten volumes. The *Phrenological Magazine* of London, edited by A. T. Story, which ran from 1880 to 1896, was incorporated with the *Phrenological Journal* of New York in the latter year.

[24] Karl Pearson, *The Life, Letters and Labours of Francis Galton*. See especially volume 2, pages 87–125 for discussion of inherited traits and eugenics and pages 285–307 for Galton's work on composite photography and archetypes. See also F. Galton, *Hereditary Genius*.

[25] Among the other relevant works of Lombroso from the physiognomical point of view are *L'Anthropologie criminelle* and *Criminal Man*, edited by Gina Lombroso-Ferrero.

[26] See Aschaffenberg, *Crime and Its Repression*, translated by Adalbert Albrecht, originally published in Germany in 1903.

[27] Redfield, *Comparative Physiognomy or Resemblances Between Men and Animals*, pages 253–58.

[28] Ibid., pages 257–58.

[29] Eden Warwick, *Nasology: Or, Hints Towards a Classification of Noses*. The real name of this connoisseur was George Jabet, who also wrote *Notes on Noses*. Unfortunately, there is not

enough space to discuss the strong narcissistic element in physiognomy, but the note of self-admiration that runs through many of these treatises should not be ignored. In Dr. Joseph Sims's book, *Physiognomy Illustrated; Or Nature's Revelations of Character* (London, 1872), which reached its ninth American edition in 1889, the final chapter is entitled "Perfection of Character." Under this same heading, there appears on the last page (page 586) a portrait of Dr. Sims, "the author of this book." Another interesting contribution from America to this field was Mary O. Stanton, *Physiognomy, A Practical and Scientific Treatise* (San Francisco, 1881).

[30] The original edition of Mantegazza's book, *La Physionomie et l'Expression des Sentiments* was translated into English and published in London in 1890 as part of Havelock Ellis's *The Contemporary Science Series.*

[31] For a good example of the hierarchy of races drawn in an arboreal form, see Figure 3.

[32] To compile a long list of these Victorian ethnohistorians and ethnographers here would serve no purpose, but among the more interesting books on the subject are: the Reverend Thomas Price, *An Essay on the Physiognomy and Physiology of the Present Inhabitants of Britain* (London, 1829); Sir William Betham, *The Gael and Cymbri* (Dublin, 1834); James C. Prichard, *The Eastern Origin of the Celtic Nations* (London, 1857); Luke Owen Pike, *The English and their Origin* (London, 1866); Thomas Wright, *The Celt, the Roman, and the Saxon* (London, 1875, 3d edition); Edwin Guest, *Origines Celticae* (London, 1883); Sir John Lubbock et al., *Mr. Gladstone and the Nationalities of the United Kingdom* (London, 1887); and Nottidge C. Macnamara, *Origin and Character of the British People* (London, 1900).

[33] *Analytical Ethnology: The Mixed Tribes in Great Britain and Ireland Examined and the Political, Physical, and Metaphysical Blunderings on the Celt and the Saxon Exposed.*

[34] Ibid., pages 5–7. These extracts are taken from a letter written by Massy just after reading Robert Knox's anti-Celtic fulminations in his *Lectures on the Races of Man*. Massy's letter was published in *The Medical Times* in November 1848 and then reprinted verbatim at the beginning of this volume.

[35] Ibid., page 157.

[36] Mackintosh, "The Comparative Anthropology of England and Wales," *Anthropological Review and Journal* (hereafter cited as *ARJ*), volume 4, pages 15–16. Darwin was quite impressed by some of Mackintosh's geological work in the late 1870s. See Francis Darwin, editor, *The Life and Letters of Charles Darwin*, 1959 reprint, volume 2, pages 410–11.

[37] Mackintosh, op. cit. (footnote 36), pages 15–16.

[38] Ibid., page 17.

[39] The notions, as distinct from systematic theories, of a number of Victorian ethnologists about the inheritance of racial and ethnic traits overlapped in places with Francis Galton's theory that the physical and mental traits of mankind were transmitted from one generation to the next through the gemmules in the bloodstream. Galton did not accept Darwin's premises and conclusions about the inheritance of acquired characteristics, but he was too much the loyal nephew and disciple of the "master" to make a public attack on the Darwinian version of pangenesis. See Karl Pearson, op. cit. (footnote 24), volume 2, pages 156–92.

[40] The Reverend W. Webster, "On Certain Points Concerning the Origin and Relations of the Basque Race," *Journal of the Anthropological Institute of Great Britain and Ireland* (hereafter cited as *JAI*). volume 2, pages 150–57. See also Webster's paper, "The Basque and the Kelt," in volume 5, pages 5–20.

[41] Hector Maclean, "Race in History," *ARJ*, volume 5, pages 129–41. Maclean was local secretary of the Anthropology Society of London in the Hebrides during the 1860s.

[42] See Hector Maclean, "On the Kimmerian and Atlantean Races," *JAI*, volume 1, pages xl–lv. Other perspectives on the subject may be found in A. L. Lewis, "Kimmerians and Atlanteans," *JAI*, volume 1, page 264; J. F. Campbell, "Kimmerians and Atlanteans," *JAI*, volume 2, pages 130–31; J. W. Jackson, "The Atlantean Race of Western Europe," *JAI*, volume 2, pages 397–402. See also J. W. Jackson, "On the Racial Aspects of the Franco–Prussian War," *JAI*, volume 1, pages 30–43.

[43] Biographical information about Beddoe may be found in the *Dictionary of National Biography, 1901–1911*, pages 124–25 and in his autobiography, *Memories of Eighty Years.*

[44] See E. A. Hooton and C. W. Dupertuis, *The Physical Anthropology of Ireland*, pages 222–223, wherein Beddoe is described as "perspicacious" and the author of a "classic work." Beddoe deserves some credit for not having accepted the popular myth that the dark hair, blue

eyes, and swarthy complexion of the Irish people derived from the procreating efforts of Spanish sailors shipwrecked on the northern and western coasts of Ireland after the defeat of the Great Armada. For a more recent refutation of this myth see Garrett Mattingly, *The Armada*, pages 368–70.

[45] Op. cit. (footnote 21), page 5.

[46] According to a content analysis of *The Times* of London, carried out under my supervision by Mr. Ken Kann, the percentage of Irish news devoted to those agrarian and political offenses which the government classified as "Special Crime" was consistently higher than such categories as agriculture, education, commerce, and finance during the 1880s. In that decade, "Special Crime" made up some 35 percent of all Irish news items in the newspaper as compared with Irish agriculture and land, the second largest category, amounting to 22 percent. In the year 1888 these two categories stood at 50 percent and 11 percent respectively in terms of all news devoted to Ireland exclusive of editorials.

[47] See the writings of Ernst Kris on caricature in *Psychoanalytic Explorations in Art* and his survey with E. H. Gombrich, *Caricature*. In addition one should consult Lawrence A. Streicher, "David Low and the Sociology of Caricature," *Comparative Studies in Society and History*, volume 8, number 2, pages 1–23, as well as his suggestive article, "On a Theory of Political Caricature," in volume 9, number 4, pages 427–45; and also W. A. Coupe, "The German Cartoon and the Revolution of 1848," in volume 9, number 2, pages 137–67. The paucity of biographical and autobiographical material bearing on the lives of Victorian cartoonists less prominent than Leech, Cruikshank, and Tenniel raises a serious obstacle to the in-depth studies that Mr. Streicher and others would like to see.

[48] Quoted in J. A. Hammerton, *Humorists of the Pencil*, pages 18–19.

[49] Information about James Gillray and his work may be found in Thomas Wright, editor, *The Works of James Gillray, The Caricaturist*, and Draper Hill, *Mr. Gillray*. See also the valuable reference work done by M. Dorothy George in *English Political Caricature: A Study of Opinions and Propaganda*.

[50] The business side of *Punch's* early years receives some mention in Marion H. Spielmann, *The History of "Punch,"* pages 30–40.

[51] Ibid., pages 62–87, 168–71.

[52] Quoted in Morton Keller, *The Art and Politics of Thomas Nast*, page 4.

[53] See especially the faces of Irish kerne, the lightly armed retainers of Irish chiefs, in some of the woodcuts in the handsome 1883 edition.

[54] Some of these prints by Gillray may be found in Wright, op. cit. (footnote 49), pages 204–05, 236–37.

[55] Ibid., pages 242–43. For another example of prognathous Irish rebels, see Gillray's "United Irishmen in Training," which is reproduced in Thomas Pakenham, *The Year of Liberty*, facing page 65.

[56] See George, op. cit. (footnote 49), volume 2, page 184 and plate 72. Additional information about the Cruikshank family may be found in Ruari McLean, *George Cruikshank, His Life and Work as a Book Illustrator*.

[57] Spielmann, op. cit. (footnote 50), pages 105–06.

[58] *Punch*, volume 5, page 199.

[59] Leech's cartoon, reproduced here, was published in *Punch* (1843), volume 4, page 37. For details of Leech's life, see *Dictionary of National Biography* (London, 1909), pages 829–32 and also Spielmann, op. cit. (footnote 50).

[60] *Punch* (8 April 1848), volume 14, page 147.

[61] See Leech's "The Battle of Limerick," ibid., page 200, and his "The Irish Ranters" on page 139. In an article in the same issue, entitled "Emblem for Ireland," Mr. Punch suggested that Ireland's national animal ought to be the hyena: "the creature—according to Wombwell's natural history—'wot kindness cannot conciliate, nor hunger tame,'" page 138.

[62] See "'My Lord Assassin' Clarendon Murdering the Irish." *Punch* (8 July 1848), volume 15, page 17; and "Alfred the Small," on page 121.

[63] This undated volume was published as a mini-pocket-book for popular consumption during or just after the Queen's first visit to Ireland in August 1849.

[64] The first edition of Maxwell's book was published in London by Baily in 1845 and the second edition by Bell in 1891.

[65] See especially the illustrations "The Murder of George Crawford and his Granddaughter" facing page 66 and "The Loyal Little Drummer" facing page 115 in the 1894 reprint of Maxwell's book.

[66] In the absence of any comprehensive biography of Tenniel, one must lean on the facts and impressions about the man which are found in the *Dictionary of National Biography, 1912–1921* (London, 1927), pages 524–26; Cosmo Monkhouse, "The Life and Artistic Achievement of Sir John Tenniel, R.I." in the Easter 1901 number of *The Art Journal*; Spielmann, op. cit. (footnote 50), pages 461–74; and Frances Sarzano, *Sir John Tenniel*.

[67] These three cartoons appeared in *Punch* respectively as follows: volume 53 (12 October 1867, pages 148–49; volume 52 (8 June 1867), page 235; and volume 53 (28 December 1867), page 263.

[68] Ibid., volume 54 (4 January 1868), page 5.

[69] Ibid., volume 81 (29 October 1881), page 199 and volume 82 (20 May 1882), page 235.

[70] "The Irish Devil-Fish" was reproduced in *Mr. Punch's Victorian Era* (London, 1887), page 151. For other examples of Tenniel's Irish stereotype, see *Punch*, volume 81: "The Rivals" (13 August 1881), page 67; "The Inferno" (17 December 1881), page 283; and "Time's Waxworks" (31 December 1881), page 307, and reproduced here as Figure 4. In volume 82 see also the frontispiece, page i; "A New Departure" (13 May 1882), page 223; and "Arrears" (3 June 1882), page 259.

[71] Sarzano, op. cit. (footnote 66), page 56. This hitherto unpublished drawing is in the possession of Sir Harold Hartley.

[72] Tenniel, "Crowning the O'Caliban," *Punch*, volume 85 (22 December 1883), page 295.

[73] There are a few, fleeting remarks about Proctor in J. A. Hammerton, op. cit. (footnote 48), pages 54–60.

[74] Ibid., page 56.

[75] *Judy*, volume 1 (9 October 1867), pages 310–11.

[76] Ibid., volume 2 (1 January 1868), page 131.

[77] Ibid., volume 2 (15 January 1868), page 155.

[78] Ibid., volume 1 (23 October 1867), pages 336–37.

[79] See volumes 28 and 29 for the year 1881.

[80] See volume 30 for January–June 1882. After July 1882, the number of specifically Irish cartoons fell off as the Egyptian question came to the fore.

[81] *Judy*, volume 28 (8 June 1881), pages 270–71.

[82] Ibid. volume 29 (26 October 1881), pages 186–87.

[83] These two sketches by Chasemore appeared in *Judy* respectively as follows: volume 31 (18 October 1882), page 190, and volume 28 (18 May 1881), page 229.

[84] Subtitled "Being a Selection, Side-Splitting, Sentimental, and Serious, for the Benefit of Old Boys, Young Boys, Odd Boys Generally, and even Girls," this comic weekly was edited by Gilbert Dalziel and published by W. J. Sinkins. A number of simianized Irishmen appear in volumes 2 and 3. See in particular the sketch of a Fenian in volume 1 (12 July 1884), page 86. English criminals were also given projecting mouths and huge jaws by some of the comic artists in this periodical. For an Irishman with more regular features, see "Only a Half-Show," volume 2 (14 November 1885), page 368.

[85] *Funny Folks*, volume 7 (22 January 1881). This periodical described itself as "The Comic Companion to the Newspaper" and as "A Weekly Budget of Funny Pictures."

[86] Ibid., volume 7 (11 June 1881).

[87] *Fun* was edited by Tom Hood and published by Cassell's Charles Whyte. After 1901, *Fun* merged with *Sketchy Bits*. Relatively few simianized Paddies appeared in *Fun* until the advent of the Irish land war in the late 1870s and early 1880s.

[88] *Dictionary of American Biography*, volume 13, pages 185–86. Graham Everitt in his *English Caricaturists and Graphic Humourists of the Nineteenth Century*, page 368, wrote that the cartoons of the *Tomahawk* "are certainly the most powerful and outspoken satires which have appeared since the days of Gillray," and he described the periodical as "superior in some important respects to *Punch*."

[89] *The Tomahawk, A Saturday Journal of Satire*, volume 5 (18 December 1869), pages 278–279.

90 Ibid., volume 6 (15 January 1870), pages 20–21.

91 Ibid., volume 1 (12 October 1867), page 235, for Morgan's "St. Dragon and the George"; and volume 6 (26 March 1870), pages 120–21, "The Odds Against Him."

92 Reproduced in *Mr. Punch's Victorian Era*, page 122.

93 Matt Morgan also gave Gladstone facial angles of 84° in "Too Strong for Them!", *The Tomahawk* (21 May 1870), page 200; and of 81° in "Grinding Away," ibid. (23 April 1870), pages 160–61.

94 These examples were chosen more or less at random from Tenniel's cartoons where good profiles were available. They may be found in the following numbers of *Punch*: Russell in "Johnny Russell's Last Job," volume 45, page 99; Gladstone in "The Political Tailors," volume 52, page 193, and "The Old Horse," volume 81, page 235; and Disraeli in "Heads I Win, Tails You Lose," volume 52, page 77. In this latter cartoon, Gladstone has an angle of 87° or 13° more than Disraeli. Some notion of Tenniel's preferences may be formed from the following order of facial angles used in *Punch*: 86° for J. S. Mill in "The Ladies' Advocate," volume 52 (1 June 1867), page 225; 75° for Abraham Lincoln in "Extremes Meet" (24 October 1863), page 169; and 67° for the Negro "Jim Crow" in "The Black Conscription" (26 September 1863), page 129. All that is required to measure facial angles may be summed up as: tracing paper, a protractor, and patience.

95 These measurements are based on the illustrations in Walter Klinefelter, *Sherlock Holmes in Portrait and Profile*.

96 See *Superboy Coloring Book*. In the comic book, *Walt Disney's Comics and Stories*, the brutish gangsters called "The Beagle Boys" have facial angles of roughly 58° compared with Superman's 82° to 90°.

97 Details of Furniss's life may be found in the *Dictionary of National Biography, 1922–1930*, pages 326–27, and also in Hammerton, op. cit. (footnote 48), pages 12–20.

98 *Punch*, volume 105, page 96.

99 Spielmann, op. cit. (footnote 50), pages 553–55.

100 *Punch*, volume 105, page 118.

101 Ibid., page 143.

102 Spielmann, op. cit. (footnote 50), page 555. See also Furniss's "A Parliamentary Bear-Garden," *Punch*, volume 105 (22 July 1893), page 35, and "Angels in the House," ibid. (29 July 1893), page 47.

103 A discussion of Nast's radical **republicanism** appears in Keller, op. cit. (footnote 52), chapter 5.

104 For these simianized Irish-Americans drawn by Nast, see *Harper's Weekly*, volume 14 (22 January 1870), pages 56–57, and ibid. (5 November 1870), page 713.

105 Ibid., volume 20 (9 December 1876), page 1069.

106 *Dictionary of American Biography*, volume 10, pages 352–53. See also H. C. Bunner, *A Selection of Cartoons from Puck by Joseph Keppler* (New York, 1893).

107 *Dictionary of American Biography*, volume 19, pages 335–36.

108 Ibid., volume 7, pages 286–87.

109 These cartoons appear in *Puck*, volume 10, pages 40–41, 220–21, and page 309, respectively.

110 Ibid., volume 8 (16 February 1881), page 395, and volume 9 (16 March 1881), pages 26–27.

111 No more than three of Dublin's cartoonists are even mentioned in Walter G. Strickland, *A Dictionary of Irish Artists*.

112 O'Hea presumably belonged to the family of that name connected with Aghamilla Castle and Kilbrittain, County Cork.

113 See *Irish Pleasantry and Fun, A Selection of the Best Humorous Tales by Carleton, Lover, Lever and Other Popular Writers*. O'Hea also illustrated part of *Gem Selection Songs of Ireland*.

114 *Zozimus*, volume 1, page 43. O'Hea also drew a prognathous Protestant evangelist trying to convert some good Catholic peasants with the aid of soup in "Connemara Neophytes," ibid. (15 June 1870), page 60.

115 *Pat*, volume 1, number 6 (7 February 1880).

116 Ibid., volume 1, number 8 (28 February 1880).

114

[117] Further details of Percy French's career may be seen in Mrs. DeBurgh Daly, *Chronicles and Poems of Percy French*, passim.

[118] Quoted in *The Dublin Figaro*, volume 1 (9 April 1892), page 115.

[119] *The Jarvey*, volume 1 (9 February 1889), page 93.

[120] Moynan merits an entry in Strickland, op. cit. (footnote 111), volume 2, pages 143–46. *The Unionist* usually carried a small and rather crudely executed black-and-white sketch on its front page.

[121] For some good examples of Erin in Irish cartoons, see the following supplements to *The Weekly Freeman*: "In Their True Colours" (31 October 1885); "Flirting Again" (26 December 1885); "Erin's Ultimatum" (10 April 1886); and "A St. Patrick's Day Reflection" (17 March 1888).

[122] Some of the most angelic features in Irish cartoons were drawn by J. D. Reigh, when he portrayed the members of the Irish parliamentary party in the weekly supplement to *United Ireland* during 1885. In his "The Conventions" (10 October 1885), Reigh drew dark-haired Erin, standing close to the noble figure of Parnell, reviewing the loyal Irish county conventions on the eve of the general election. See also his double-page illustration, "The Irish Benches— The Irish Parliamentary Party of 1885," ibid. (24 December 1885).

[123] *The Weekly News* supplement varied from 8.4 x 10.1 inches to 12.4 x 9.2 inches in 1884. *The Weekly Freeman* supplement measured 8.5 x 9.9 inches in 1883 and 10 x 16.5 inches in 1884; and one number in 1892 measured 20.1 x 13.3 inches. The St. Patrick's Day number for *The Weekly Freeman and National Press* in 1902 was 19.5 x 15.8 inches. Similar variations may be found in the other weekly color supplements.

[124] J. D. Reigh drew a number of ugly, brutish Orangemen in *United Ireland's* weekly supplement, among the best examples being, "Orange Swashbuckler" (5 January 1884); "An Even Keel" (26 January 1884); and "Orange Prudence and Self-Denial" (14 June 1884). An informer with brutish features appears in his "After the Job" (5 April 1884).

[125] In "The Original and the Copy," *Weekly Freeman* (24 January 1885), the artist (presumably O'Hea) drew Joseph Chamberlain standing on a Radical platform, dated 1885, holding a red banner and addressing his prognathous constituents. In the background stands Parnell, holding a green banner and speaking to his orthognathous followers from a Land League platform, dated 1880.

[126] Unlike O'Hea, "Fitz" receives a brief biographical sketch in Strickland, op. cit. (footnote 111), volume 1, pages 352–53. A few more impressions and details appear in the tribute paid to him in *The Lepracaun* (July 1912), volume 8, pages 25 and 32.

[127] See for example Fitzpatrick's "The Colleen Bawn at Westminster" (August 1908), page 57; and "The Treaty Stone" (April 1911), page 157. Other unflattering versions of John Bull appear in the numbers for May and July 1907, April 1908, and November 1909.

[128] Ibid. (October 1911), page 231.

[129] *The Weekly Freeman and National Press* (7 January 1893).

[130] Ibid. (29 April 1893).

[131] *The Irish Pilot*, volume 1, pages 28–29.

[132] *The Weekly Freeman and National Press* (10 June 1905).

[133] See Ernest Kavanagh, *Cartoons: The Redmond–O'Brien Press Gang*. See especially "Worker and Sweater" and "Birrell's Bullies."

[134] This account of the explosive cartoon is based on *The Irish Times*, 8–10 May 1893; and M. McD. Bodkin to W. E. Gladstone, 20 March 1894, the Gladstone Papers, British Museum, Add. MSS 44, 518, ff. 124–25.

[135] See Mantle Fielding's *Dictionary of American Painters, Sculptors, and Engravers with an addendum containing corrections and additional material on the original entries compiled by James F. Carr*, page 263.

[136] *The Illustrated London News*, volume 78 (5 February 1881), pages 146–47; (21 May 1881), page 493; and (18 June 1881), pages 612–13 respectively. See also in *The Illustrated London News*, volume 78, O'Kelly's "The State of Ireland: Tilling the Farm of an Imprisoned Land Leaguer" (7 May 1881), page 452; and "An Eviction in the West of Ireland" (19 March 1881), pages 290–91.

[137] *The Illustrated London News*, volume 78 (22 January 1881), pages 80–81. For other fine features on Irish faces, the 8 January 1881 issue contains the work of an anonymous special

artist "The Irish Land League Trials in Dublin: Traversers Leaving the Court" on page 25, and F. Dadd, "The Irish Land League: Mr. Boynton Burning the Duke of Leinster's Leases" on page 29. See also Woodville's "Souvenir d'Irlande—Une scene populaire sur la route de Connemara" in *L'Univers Illustré* of 7 February 1880.

138 The illustrations by Montbard and Forestier in the March 1885 number of *L'Univers Illustré* depict Irish peasant faces in a flattering manner.

139 *The Graphic*, volume 31 (25 April 1885), page 400.

140 See for example, "Irish Sketches—Turf Carriers," ibid., volume 1 (6 March 1870), page 385; and "The Wandering Heir," Christmas number (25 December 1872), page 4. For the coverage of the Phoenix Park murders, see volume 25 (13 May 1882), pages 469 and 472.

141 These photographs may be found in the prison files which constitute one portion of the Fenian Papers at the State Paper Office, Dublin Castle.

142 Reproductions of the prison photographs of John O'Leary, John Haltigan, Thomas Clarke Luby, and Denis Dowling Mulcahy, taken at Mountjoy jail, Dublin, in 1865, appear in Marcus Bourke, *John O'Leary, A Study in Irish Separatism*, facing page 81.

143 This photograph was first published in *Sights and Scenes in Ireland*, page 173, and has been reproduced in T. W. Moody and F. X. Martin, editors, *The Course of Irish History*, page 225.

144 Hooton and Dupertuis, op. cit. (footnote 44), page 66, and table IV—42 to 44.

145 For the significance of these contradictory attributes, see L. P. Curtis Jr, op. cit. (footnote 2), pages 49–65, 100–07.

146 This quotation from Pinkerton (1758–1826) appeared in an essay in *The Anti-Jacobin Review*, volume 32, number 129 (March 1809), page 243. The Celtophobia of "the fretful Pinkerton" may be seen in its most concentrated form in his *A Dissertation on the Origin and Progress of the Scythians or Goths*.

147 Moriarty, the ex-professor of mathematics and doubtless the most evil man in London, was evidently inspired by several of Conan Doyle's teachers at Edinburgh, just as Holmes reflected a good deal of the notable surgeon, Joseph Bell, who taught the writer in medical school. The Celtic background and Saxon foreground of Conan Doyle is discussed briefly in Pierre Nordon, *Sir Arthur Conan Doyle*, chapters 1 and 2.

148 The following paragraphs about anti-Irish and anti-Catholic prejudices in Scotland owe much to the work of James E. Handley, *The Irish in Modern Scotland*, in particular, chapter 5.

149 Ibid., page 105.

150 Ibid., page 108.

151 Ibid., page 263.

152 *Apes and Ape Lore in the Middle Ages and the Renaissance*.

153 *Encyclopaedia Britannica*, eighth edition (Edinburgh, 1856–57), volume 14, pages 137–44. One footnote (page 137) in the article on the simiidae is worth quoting because of its relevance to the facial angle: "In accordance with the usual custom of naturalists, we here occasionally indicate the facial angle, although we are satisfied that that character admits of too wide a range of variation to be relied upon as a specific indication. An examination of an extensive series of skulls in the Museum of the College of Surgeons (Edinburgh) had long ago convinced us that remarkable changes take place in the form and proportions of the cranium in the same species, according to the age of different individuals." The author listed the facial angle of the "Genus *Troglodytes*" (the "only known species of this genus" being the chimpanzee) as 50°; and the "Genus *Pithecus*" (meaning here the Asiatic orangutan) was given an angle of 65°.

154 *Encyclopaedia Britannica*, ninth edition (Edinburgh, 1875), volume 2, pages 148–69. The author of the article on "Apes," Mivart, made no mention of facial angles in the manner of his predecessor.

155 *Fun*, volume 1, page 7.

156 Ibid. (19 October 1861), page 44.

157 Ibid. (11 January 1862), page 166.

158 Ibid. (8 March 1862), page 249.

159 *Punch*, volume 43 (18 March 1862), page 165.

160 Frances E. Kingsley, editor, *Charles Kingsley, His Letters and Memories of His Life*, volume 2, page 107.

161 *The Strand Magazine*, volume 3 (January–June 1892), page 32.

[162] Some acutely prognathous and brutish criminals, cousins in several respects of the simianized version of Paddy, may be seen in J. F. Sullivan, *The British Working Man*. See especially, "A Truly Terrible Punishment," page 56, and "Among the Savages," page 55. A prognathous criminal appears in W. Bowcher's cartoon, "School (?) *versus* Jail," *Judy* (30 November 1881), pages 246–47.

[163] See the tribute paid to Pellegrini on his death in *Vanity Fair*, volume 41 (26 January 1889), page 55.

[164] Thomas Finn of Carlow wrote this public letter, "To Mr. Daniel O'Connell" which was printed in Cork in 1835 by Barry Drew. In the course of his diatribe, Finn suggested that O'Connell was descended from "one of those Antropophagi [sic] New Zealanders whom you resemble so much." Ibid., page 4.

[165] An informed and witty study of the Darwinian controversy is the work by the late William Irvine, *Apes, Angels, and Victorians*. The full title of Darwin's classic work is worth quoting, if only because a number of impressionable Victorians may not have ventured very far beyond the title page: *On the Origin of Species by Means of Natural Selection, or the Preservation of Favoured Races in the Struggle for Life.*

[166] See Huxley's own account in *Man's Place in Nature*, pages v–xii and chapters 1–2.

[167] *The Descent of Man and Selection in Relation to Sex.* The quotation comes from page 153 of the 1889 edition.

[168] Sir Christopher Lynch-Robinson, *The Last of the Irish R.M.'s*, page 160.

[169] Ibid.

[170] See Figure 46. Tenniel's cartoon appeared in *Punch*, volume 47 (10 December 1864), page 239. Disraeli's facial angle here comes close to 78°.

[171] This is the abbreviated as well as corrupt version of Gregory's famous response: " 'Bene,' inquit; 'nam et angelicam habent faciem, et tales angelorum in caelis decet esse coheredes.' " Bede, *Historia Ecclesiastica*, book 2, chapter 1. Pope Gregory had asked the name of this "race" of islanders, and he was told that they were called Angles. "That is appropriate," he said, "for they have angelic faces, and it is right that they should become joint-heirs with the angels in heaven." From Bede, *A History of the English Church and People*. Revised edition. Translated by Leo Sherley-Price. Harmondsworth: Penguin Books, 1968, page 100.

Selected Bibliography

Aristotle. *The History of Animals of Aristotle and His Treatise on Physiognomy.* Translated by Thomas Taylor. London, 1809.

Aschaffenberg, Gustav. *Crime and Its Repression.* Translated by Adalbert Albrecht. Boston: Little, Brown & Co., 1913. [Originally published in Germany in 1903.]

Beddoe, John. *Memories of Eighty Years.* Bristol: J. W. Arrowsmith, 1910.

————. *The Races of Britain, A Contribution to the Anthropology of Western Europe.* Bristol: J. W. Arrowsmith, and London: Trubner, 1885.

Bell, Sir Charles. *Essays on the Anatomy of Expression in Painting.* London: Longmans & Company, 1806.

Bendyshe, Thomas, translator and editor. *The Anthropological Treatises of Johann Friedrich Blumenbach.* London, 1865.

Betham, Sir William. *The Gael and Cymbri.* Dublin: W. Curry & Company, 1834.

Bourke, Marcus. *John O'Leary, A Study in Irish Separatism.* Tralee: Anvil Books, 1967.

Campbell, J. F. "Kimmerians and Atlanteans," *Journal of the Anthropological Institute of Great Britain and Ireland,* volume 2 (1873), pages 130–31.

Cherry, Samuel and Anna. *Otyognomy, Or the External Ear as an Index to Character.* New York: The Neely Company, 1900.

Cogan, T., editor. *The Works of the Late Professor Camper on the Connection between the Science of Anatomy and the Arts of Drawing, Painting, Statuary.* London: C. Dilly, 1794.

Conan Doyle, A. *The Adventures and Memoirs of Sherlock Holmes.* New York: Modern Library, 1946.

Coupe, W. A. "The German Cartoon and the Revolution of 1848," *Comparative Studies in Society and History,* volume 9, number 2 (January 1967).

Curtis, L. P., Jr. *Anglo-Saxons and Celts: A Study of Anti-Irish Prejudice in Victorian England.* Bridgeport, Connecticut: Conference on British Studies, 1968.

Daly, Mrs. DeBurgh. *Chronicles and Poems of Percy French.* Dublin: Talbot Press, 1922.

Darwin, Charles. *The Descent of Man and Selection in Relation to Sex.* London: Murray, 1871.

————. *The Expression of the Emotions in Man and Animals.* London: John Murray, 1872. New York, 1896.

————. *On the Origin of Species by Means of Natural Selection, or the Preservation of Favoured Races in the Struggle for Life.* London: Murray, 1859.

Darwin, Francis, editor. *The Life and Letters of Charles Darwin.* Three volumes, 1887. Reprinted, New York: Johnson Reprint Corporation, 1959.

Davies, John D. *Phrenology, Fad and Science.* New Haven: Yale University Press, 1955.

Della Porta, Giovanni Battista. *De Humana Physiognomonia.* Hanoviae, 1593.

Derricke, John. *The Image of Irelande with a Discouerie of Woodkarne.* Edinburgh: A. and C. Black, 1883.

Duchenne, G. B. A. *Mécanisme de la Physionomie humaine.* Paris, 1862.

Everitt, Graham. *English Caricaturists and Graphic Humourists of the Nineteenth Century.* London: Swan Sonnenschein, 1886.

Fielding, Mantle. *Dictionary of American Painters, Sculptors, and Engravers with an Addendum Containing Corrections and Additional Material on the Original Entries Compiled by James F. Carr.* New York: James F. Carr, 1965.

Galton, Francis. *Hereditary Genius.* London: Macmillan & Company, 1869.
Gem Selection Songs of Ireland. Dublin: Valentine, no date.
George, M. Dorothy. *English Political Caricature: A Study of Opinions and Propaganda.* Two volumes. Oxford: Clarendon Press, 1959.
Gratiolet, Louis Pierre. *De la Physionomie et des Mouvements d'Expression.* Paris, 1865.
Guest, Edwin. *Origines Celticae.* Two volumes. London: Macmillan & Company, 1883.

Hall, Mrs S. C. *Tales of Irish Life and Character.* London: T. N. Foulis, 1909.
Hammerton, J. A. *Humorists of the Pencil.* London: Hurst and Blackett, 1905.
Handley, James E. *The Irish in Modern Scotland.* Cork: Cork University Press, 1947.
Hartenberg, Paul. *Physionomie et Caractère.* Paris, 1908.
Hill, Draper. *Mr. Gillray.* London: Phaidon Press, 1965.
Hippocrates. *Works.* Translated by W. H. S. Jones. Volume 4. Cambridge: Harvard University Press, 1959.
Hooton, E. A., and Dupertuis, C. W. *The Physical Anthropology of Ireland.* Cambridge, Massachusetts: The Peabody Museum, 1955.
Huxley, Thomas. *Man's Place in Nature.* New York: D. Appleton & Company, 1896.

Irish Pleasantry and Fun, A Selection of the Best Humorous Tales by Carleton, Lover, Lever and Other Popular Writers. Dublin: M. H. Gill, 1882.
Irvine, William. *Apes, Angels, and Victorians.* New York: McGraw-Hill Book Company, 1955.

Jabet, George (pseudonym, Eden Warwick). *Nasology: Or Hints Towards a Classification of Noses.* London, 1848.
————. *Notes on Noses.* London, 1852.
Jackson, J. W. "The Atlantean Race of Western Europe," *Journal of the Anthropological Institute of Great Britain and Ireland,* volume 2 (1873), pages 397–402.
————. "On the Racial Aspects of the Franco-Prussian War," *Journal of the Anthropological Institute of Great Britain and Ireland,* volume 1 (1872), pages 30–43.
Janson, Horst W. *Apes and Ape Lore in the Middle Ages and the Renaissance.* London: Warburg Institute, 1952.
Jordan, Winthrop D., editor. *An Essay on the Causes of the Variety of Complexion and Figure in the Human Species by Samuel Stanhope Smith.* Cambridge: Harvard University Press, 1965.

Kavanagh, Ernest. *Cartoons: The Redmond-O'Brien Press Gang.* Dublin, no date [1917?].
Keller, Morton. *The Art and Politics of Thomas Nast.* New York: Oxford University Press, 1968.
Kingsley, Frances E., editor. *Charles Kingsley, His Letters and Memories of His Life.* London: H. S. King, 1877.

Klinefelter, Walter. *Sherlock Holmes in Portrait and Profile.* New York: Syracuse University Press, 1963.

Kris, Ernst. *Psychoanalytic Explorations in Art.* New York: International Universities Press, Inc., 1952.

Kris, Ernst, and Gombrich, E. H. *Caricature.* Baltimore: Penguin Books, 1940.

Lavater, Johann Kaspar. *Essays on Physiognomy For the Promotion of the Knowledge and Love of Mankind.* Translated by Thomas Holcroft. London: G. and J. Robinson, 1789.

Lawless, Emily. *Hurrish, A Study.* Two volumes. Edinburgh: William Blackwood, 1886.

Leigh, Denis. *The Historical Development of British Psychiatry.* Volume 1. London: Pergamon, 1961.

Lewis, A. L. "Kimmerians and Atlanteans," *Journal of the Anthropological Institute of Great Britain and Ireland,* volume 1 (1872).

Lombroso, Cesare. *L'Anthropologie criminelle.* 2nd edition, Paris, 1891.

————. *Criminal Man.* Edited by Gina Lombroso-Ferrero. New York: G. P. G. P. Putnam's Sons, 1911.

————. *L'Uomo delinquente.* Milano, 1876.

Lubbock, Sir John, et al. *Mr. Gladstone and the Nationalities of the United Kingdom.* London: Bernard Quaritch, 1887.

Lynch-Robinson. Sir Christopher. *The Last of the Irish R.M.'s.* London: Cassell and Company, 1951.

Macalister, Alexander. "Physiognomy," in *Encyclopaedia Britannica.* 11th edition, volume 21, pages 550–552. New York, 1911.

Mackintosh, Daniel. "The Comparative Anthropology of England and Wales," *Anthropological Review and Journal,* volume 4 (1866).

Maclean, Hector. "Race in History," *Anthropological Review and Journal.* Volume 5. London, 1866.

Maclean, Hector. "On the Kimmerian and Atlantean Races," *Journal of the Anthropological Institute of Great Britain and Ireland,* volume 1 (1872), pages xl–lv.

McLean, Ruari. *George Cruikshank, His Life and Work as a Book Illustrator.* London: Art and Technics, 1948.

Macnamara, Nottidge C. *Origin and Character of the British People.* London: Smith, Elder & Company, 1900.

Mantegazza, Paolo. *Physiognomy and Expression.* London: Walter Scott, 1890. [Translation.]

————. *La Physionomie et l'Expression des Sentiments.* Paris: Versailles, 1885.

Massy, Richard Tuthill. *Analytical Ethnology: The Mixed Tribes in Great Britain and Ireland Examined and the Political, Physical, and Metaphysical Blunderings on the Celt and the Saxon Exposed.* London: H. Bailliere and Bath: Binns & Goodwin, 1855.

Mattingly, Garrett. *The Armada.* Boston: Houghton Mifflin Company, 1959.

Maxwell, W. H. *History of the Rebellion in Ireland in 1798.* London: Baily, 1845; 2d edition, London: Bell, 1891; reprint, London, 1894.

Mivart, St. George. "Apes," *Encyclopaedia Britannica,* 9th edition, volume 2. Edinburgh, 1875.

Molinari, Gustave de, *L'Irlande, le Canada, Jersey.* Paris: Lagny, 1881.

Monkhouse, Cosmo. "The Life and Artistic Achievement of Sir John Tenniel, R.I.," *The Art Journal,* Easter issue, 1901.

Moody, T. W., and Martin, F. X., editors. *The Course of Irish History*. New York: Dutton, 1967.

Morris, Ramona and Desmond. *Men and Apes*. New York: McGraw-Hill Book Company, 1966.

Mr. Punch's Irish Humour. In *Punch Library of Humour* series, under general editorship of J. A. Hammerton. London: The Educational Book Company, no date [circa 1910].

Mr. Punch's Victorian Era. London, 1887.

Nordon, Pierre. *Sir Arthur Conan Doyle*. Paris: Didier, 1964.

Pakenham, Thomas. *The Year of Liberty*. London: Hodder and Stoughton, 1969.

Pearson, Karl. *The Life, Letters and Labours of Francis Galton*. Three volumes. Cambridge: Cambridge University Press, 1914–30.

Phillips, Watts. *The Queen in Ireland*. London [circa August 1849].

Phrenological Journal and Miscellany. Edinburgh, 1824–37.

Phrenological Journal and Magazine of Moral Science. New series, 10 volumes. Edinburgh, 1838–47.

Phrenological Magazine. London, 1880–96.

Pike, Luke Owen. *The English and their Origin*. London, 1866.

Pinkerton, John. *A Dissertation on the Origin and Progress of the Scythians or Goths*. London, 1787.

Preston, Adrian, editor, *In Relief of Gordon*. London: Hutchinson, 1967.

Price, Thomas. *An Essay on the Physiognomy and Physiology of the Present Inhabitants of Britain*. London, 1829.

Prichard, James Cowles. *The Eastern Origin of the Celtic Nations*. 1st edition. Oxford, 1831.

————. *Researches into the Physical History of Man*. London: J. and A. Arch, 1813.

Redfield, James W. *Comparative Physiognomy or Resemblances Between Men and Animals*. New York, 1852.

Retzius, Anders Adolph. "Present State of Ethnology in Relation to the Form of the Human Skull," *Annual Report of the Smithsonian Institution, 1859*. Washington, D.C., 1860.

Sargant, William. *The Battle for the Mind*. New York: Doubleday, 1957.

Sarzano, Frances. *Sir John Tenniel*. London: Art and Technics, 1948.

Sights and Scenes in Ireland. London: Cassell and Company, no date [1896].

Sims, Dr. Joseph. *Physiognomy Illustrated: Or Nature's Revelations of Character*. London, 1872.

Singer, Charles. *A Short History of Anatomy and Physiology from the Greeks to Harvey*. New York: Dover, 1957.

Spielmann, Marion H. *The History of "Punch."* London: Cassell, 1895.

Stanton, Mary O. *Physiognomy, A Practical and Scientific Treatise*. San Francisco, 1881.

Stanton, William R. *The Leopard's Spots: Scientific Attitudes Toward Race in America, 1815–59*. Chicago: University of Chicago Press, 1960.

Streicher, Lawrence A. "David Low and the Sociology of Caricature," *Comparative Studies in Society and History*, volume 8, number 2 (October 1965).

————. "On a Theory of Political Caricature," *Comparative Studies in Society and History*, volume 9, number 4 (July 1967).

Strickland, Walter G. *A Dictionary of Irish Artists*. Two volumes. Dublin: Maunsel and Company, 1913.

Sullivan, J. F. *The British Working Man*. London: "Fun" Office, 1878.

Trench, W. Steuart. *Ierne, A Tale*. 2d edition. London: Longmans, Green, and Company, 1871.

Warwick, Eden. See under George Jabet.

Webster, W. "The Basque and the Kelt," *Journal of the Anthropological Institute of Great Britain and Ireland*. Volume 5. London, 1876.

————. "On Certain Points Concerning the Origin and Relations of the Basque Race," *Journal of the Anthropological Institute of Great Britain and Ireland*. Volume 2. London, 1873.

Wright, Thomas. *The Celt, the Roman, and the Saxon*. 1st edition. London: Arthur Hall, Virtue & Company, 1852.

Wright, Thomas, editor. *The Works of James Gillray, The Caricaturist*. London: Chatto and Windus, 1873.

Index

Aborigines, 2, 13
"Africanoid" man in Ireland, 20, 91
Ally Sloper's Half Holiday, 27, 47, 113
anthropology, Victorian, 13–15, 17–20, 103
"Ape." *See* Pellegrini, Carlo
Aristotle, 6
Arkell, W. J., 62
Armour, George D., 57
Aschaffenberg, Gustav, 12
Ayton, A., 90, 92

Balfour, Arthur James, 77
Baxter, W. G., 47
Beaumont, Gustave de, 1
Beddoe, John, 19–20, 91, 111
Bell, Sir Charles, 7, 9–10
Blake, Phil, 76, 81
blood, associated with heredity, 17, 95, 111
Blood, A. F., 69
Blumenbach, Johann F., 7–9, 12
Bodkin, Matthias M., 83
Bonatt, L. J. F., 84
Bowcher, W., 46–47, 64, 89
Bradbury, Evans, and Agnew, publishers, 27
Brady, Mat, 4–5
Brennan, 100
Britannia, 25, 38, 41, 52, 75
Brooks, Sydney, 77
Browne, Hablot K. ("Phiz"), 4
Bull, John, 37, 40, 48, 66, 68, 76, 77, 82, 104
Burke and Hare, murderers, 97

Caesar, 19
Caliban, 2, 4–5, 20, 22, 29, 45, 68, 75, 88, 89, 101, 107
Camper, Pieter, vii, 7–11, 20, 50–52, 109
caricatura, 23

caricature, *passim*
Carroll, Lewis, 36
cartoons, *passim*, defined, 23–24
Cassell's Illustrated Family Paper, 26
Cavendish, Lord Frederick, 38
Chamberlain, Joseph, 76
Chasemore, Archibald, 47
Cherry, Anna and Samuel, 13
Chinese, 2
chromolithography, 28
Clerkenwell explosion, 37, 98
Cloncurry, Lord, 5
Cobden, Richard, 11
Colliers, Once A Week, 48
Combe, G., 11
comic books, 53, 114
Conan Doyle, Arthur, 4, 97, 116
Cornwall, 17, 20
Crane, Walter, 83
craniology, 11
Crawford, George, 35
Crawfurd, John, 13
Cruikshank, George, 26, 30, 34–37, 89, 96, 113
Cruikshank, Isaac, 30, 96
Cruikshank, Robert, 30

Darwin, Charles R., 9–10, 21, and Darwinism, 99, 101–4, 106–7, 110
Davies, Sir John, 95
Davis, J. Barnard, 11
Davis, Thomas, 31
Derricke, John, 29, 112
Dickens, Charles, 3, 4
Disraeli, Benjamin, 3, 52, 106–7
Dublin, 27, 28, 48, 68–84
Dublin Castle, Fenian Papers in, 89–91
Duchenne, G. B. A., 13
Dupertuis, C. W., 90, 93

Edinburgh, 12, 13, 45, 96–97, 99

Eliot, George, 11
emigration, the Irish in Scotland, 97–98
Erin, female symbol of Ireland, 37, 57, 65, 75, 76, 81, 88
ethnology, Victorian, 13–15, 16–21, 111
evolution, and caricature, 98–104
explosive cartoon, the affair of, 82–83

facial angle, 7–11, 20; applied to cartoons, 50–53, 55–56, 109–10, 114, 116
Fenianism, 21–22, 25, 26, 37–40, 45–46, 50, 82, 98, 101–2
Fenian physiognomies, 89–92
Fitzpatrick, Mary, 77
Fitzpatrick, Thomas, 72–73, 76–82, 89
Fleet Street, 26–27, 37, 68, 72
Four Courts, Dublin, 82–83
Fox, Charles James, 26
Frank Leslie's Illustrated Newspaper, 48, 62, 96
Frankenstein, the Irish, 22, 31–32, 38, 43, 45, 48–49, 52, 75, 79–80, 89
Freeman, E. A., 94
Freeman's Journal, 73
French, William Percy, 73
Froude, James A., 94
Fun, 27, 45, 48, 100
Funny Folks, 27, 45, 48
Furniss, Harry, 24, 54–57, 89, 96

Gaelic typology, 17–20
Galen, 6, 13
Gall, F. J., 11–12
Galton, Francis, 12, 19
Gérôme, J. L., 84
Gillam, Bernhard, 62, 64
Gillray, James, 26, 30–31, 37, 45, 96, 112
Gladstone, William E., 44–46, 52, 82–83, 97
Glasgow Herald, 98
Gobineau, J. A. de, 20
Gombrich, E. H., 28
gorillas, x, 2, 22, 31, 47, 53, 56, 82, 100–5; discovery of, 99
Gradgrind, Thomas, 4
Grant, Madison, 20
Graphic, The, 87
Gratiolet, Louis Pierre, 13

Grätz, F., 64
Gray, Paul, 48
Gregory I, Pope, 108, 117
Guy Fawkes, the Fenian, 37, 39

Hall, Sydney Prior, 87
Halliday, Henry, 82–83
Hamilton, Edwin, 69
Hanno of Carthage, 99
Harper's Weekly, 27, 58–60, 62
Hartenberg, Paul, 13
Harvey, William, 6
Hibernia, female symbol of Ireland, 25, 31, 37, 41, 46, 57, 65
Hippocrates, 5–6
Holmes, Sherlock, 4, 52, 59, 97
Home Rule, viii, 28, 69, 72, 75–77, 82–83, 87
Hooton, E. A., 90, 93
Hottentots, 2, 13
humoralism, 5–6, 10, 96, 109, 110
Hunt, James, 13, 20
Hurrish, A Tale, 4–5
Huxley, Thomas H., 21, 100, 103, 106–107

Ierne, A Tale, 3–4
Illustrated London News, The, 26, 27, 48, 83–87
Illustrated Times, The, 26
Ireland's Eye, 69, 76
Irish Cyclist, The, 73
Irish Emerald, The, 77
Irish Figaro, The, 69, 77
Irish Fireside, The, 69
Irish Freedom, 81
Irish Fun, 81–82
Irish landlords, stereotyped, 78–79
Irish newspaper color supplements, 76–83, 115
Irish Pilot, The, 76, 81
Irish Republican Brotherhood, 95
Irish Times, The, 83

Jabet, George (Eden Warwick), 13
Jacobins, caricatured, 30
Janson, Horst, W., 99
Jarvey, The, 72–75, 76
Judge, 59, 62, 64–65
Judy, vii, 27, 45–47, 94

Kalmuck, 7–8

Kames, Lord, 26
Kavanagh, Ernest ("E. K."), 81
Keene, Charles, 36, 57
Keppler, Joseph, 61–62, 64
Kilkenny cats, 46–47
Kimmerians, 19
Kingsley, Charles, 3, 94, 100
Kipling, Rudyard, 3
Knox, Robert, 20, 97

Land League, the Irish, 41, 44, 46, 48, 50, 85–86, 92
Larkin, Jim, 81
Lavater, Johann Kaspar, 7, 26, 30
Lawless, the Honorable Emily, 4–5
Leech, John, 31, 33–34, 36, 96, 100, 112
Lemon, Mark, 36
Lepracaun, The, 69, 77
Leslie, Frank, 28, 48, 62, 96
Levine, David, 53
"Lex." *See* Moynan, R. T.
Liberty Hall, 81
Lloyd, A. W., 57
Lombroso, Cesare, 12
London, 13, 26–28, 82, 87–88
Luby, T. C., 90
Lucy, Henry W., 54–55
Lynch-Robinson, Sir C., 105
Lytton, Lord, 3

Macaulay, Thomas B., 94
Mackintosh, Daniel, 17–19, 97
Maclean, Hector, 19, 97
MacNeill, John G. Swift, 54–56
Mantegazza, Paolo, 13, 14
Maoris, 2
Massy, Richard Tuthill, 16–17
Maxwell, W. H., 34, 35
May, Phil, 57
Meadows, J. Kenny, 31–32, 96
Mecredy, R. J., 73
Mills, W. C., 76
"Missing Link," 100
Mitchel, John, 34, 100
Mivart, St. George, 99
Molinari, Gustave de, 1, 109
Moonlight, Captain, 43, 87
Moonshine, 27, 45, 48
Morgan, Matthew S., 28, 48–51, 52, 75, 79, 80, 89, 96
Moriarty, Professor, 4, 97

Morris, William, 83
Moryson, Fynes, 95
Moynan, Richard Thomas, 75

Nast, Thomas, 24, 28, 48, 58–60, 64, 96
National League, the Irish, 81
National Press, The, 77
New York City, viii, 28, 48, 58–59, 62, 82, 87, 88, 96
New York Graphic, The, 62
Nigrescence, Index of, 19–20
North British Daily Mail, The, 98

O'Connell, Daniel, 32, 100, 102, 117
O'Donoghue, The, 100
O'Hea, John Fergus, 68–72, 73, 75, 76, 77, 89, 90
O'Kelly, Aloysius C., 84–86, 90
O'Leary, John, 90
O'Mahony, John, 90
Opper, Frederick B., 63–64
orangutans, 2, 4, 7–8, 31, 48, 53, 58, 82, and O'Connell, 102
Origin of Species, On the, 99–104
Orpen, Richard Caulfeild, 73–75
Orpen, Sir William, 73
Orr, John Sayers, 97
O'Shea, W. T., 76
Owen, Sir Richard, 103

Paddy, 2–3, 20–22, 29, 35, 37, 58, 61, 63, 75, 89, 94–95, 101, 107
"Paddy," the chimpanzee, 101
Paget, Sidney, 52
Parnell, Charles S., 47, 76
Partridge, Bernard, 57
Pat, 1, 72, 75–76, 78, 88
Pat, 69–72, 76, 77
pathognomy, 9–10
Pavlov, Ivan P., 109
Peel, Sir Robert, 96
Pellegrini, Carlo, 102
Penny Illustrated Paper, The, 26
Phillips, Watts, 34
Phoenix Park murders, 38, 43, 48, 87
physiognomy, viii, 1–15, 109, and *passim*, and narcissism, 111
phrenology, 11–12, 110
Pinkerton, John, 95, 97, 101
Pope, Alexander, x
Price, the Reverend Thomas, 19

Prichard, James C., 7, 10
Proctor, John, 45–46, 48, 64, 89, 96
prognathism, in Irish faces, 89–93
Protestantism, popular, 97–98
Puck, 59, 61–67
Punch, vii, 1, 23–45 *passim*, 68, 81, 94, 100, 103, 106–7, and post-1900 cartoons, 57

Quiz, The, 69

Raven-Hill, L., 57
Redfield, James W., 12–13
Redmond, John E., 77–79, 81
Reidy, Michael, 81–82
Reigh, John D., 69, 76, 77, 83, 89, 115
Retzius, Anders A., 11
Robinson, Sir Henry, 105
Ross, Charles, 45
Rowlandson, Thomas, 30
Royal Irish Constabulary, 90, 105
Russell, Lord John, 52

St. George, and the Dragon, 37, 45–46, 48, 51, 82
St. Patrick, 46
Salisbury, Lord, 79, 80
"Sancho Panza" Celts, 19, 35
Savage, Dr. Thomas S., 99
Scarfe, Gerald, 53
Schwartzmann, A., 62
Scotland, 20, 30
Scott, Sir Walter, 3
Scottish complexion of cartoonists, 96–98
Scottish Guardian, The, 98
Sinn Fein, 57, 77
Smith, Goldwin, 94
Social Darwinism, 104
Somerville, Edith, ix
Spielmann, Marion H., 31
Spencer, Earl of, 76–77
Spenser, Edmund, 95
"Spex." *See* O'Hea, J. F.
Spurzheim, J. K., 11–12
Stafford, J., 47–48
Steele, Frederick Dorr, 52
Stephens, James, 90
Strabo, 19
Strand Magazine, The, 101
Sudanese, 2, 109

Sunshine, The, 69, 76
Superboy, 53
Swan and Dalziel, engravers, 37
Swan, W. P., 72

Tacitus, 19
Tanner, Dr., 55
Teague, 2, 29
Tenniel, Sir John, 23–24, 26, 28, 35–46 *passim*, 58, 64, 69, 73, 74, 75, 81, 89, 90, 96, 106–7, 113
Thurnam, J., 11
Times, The, of London, 21, 26, 28, 94, 112
Tomahawk, The, 27, 48–51
Tomsohn and Wogan, printers, 69
Tracy, Dick, 59
Trench, W. Steuart, 3
Trinity College, Dublin, 73
Trollope, Anthony, 3
Tweed, Boss, 28, 58

Ulstermen, 79
Unionist, The, 75
United Ireland, 76, 82–83
L'Univers Illustré, 86

Vanity Fair, 102
Vesalius, 6
Victoria, Queen, 34, 87, 112

Wales, 17, 20
Wales, James Albert, 62, 66–67
Wallace, Alfred R., 21
Weekly Freeman, The, 69, 76–81
Weekly Irish Times, The, 76
Weekly Nation, The, 77
Weekly News, The, 76
Westminster, 55–56
"white Negroes," 1, 13, 15
Wilberforce, Dr. Samuel, Bishop of Oxford, 103, 107
Will-O-the-Wisp, 27, 45
Woodville, Richard Caton, 86
Worker, The, 81

Yahoo, the Irish, 69
Young Ireland, 69

Zoz, 69
Zozimus, 68–69